Ten Keys for Opening the Bible

Ten Keys for Opening the Bible

An Introduction to the First Testament

Jacques Vermeylen

Continuum • New York

2000

The Continuum International Publishing Group Inc
370 Lexington Avenue, New York, NY 10017

Translated by John Bowden from the French, *Dix clés pour ouvrir la Bible*

© Les Éditions du Cerf 1999

Translation © John Bowden 1999

Printed in Great Britain

Library of Congress Cataloging-in-Publication Data
Vermeylen, J. (Jacques)
    [Dix clés pour ouvrir la Bible, English]
    Ten keys for opening the Bible : an introduction to the First Testamen
Jacques Vermeylen.
        p.   cm.
    ISBN 0-8264-1256-4
    1. Bible. O.T. — Introductions. I. Title.

BS1140.2 V47 2000
221.6′1—dc21   99-089364

Contents

Introduction   1

1. How do we read?   5

   The foundation documents   6
   Listening for the Other   8
      Historical readings   10
      So-called 'synchronic' readings   12
   Making a covenant   13
   The Bible best read in the church   16
   By way of a conclusion   17

2. The geographical framework   19

   Geography of the ancient Near East   19
      Mesopotamia   21
      Egypt   22
      The other centres of civilization   23
   Palestinian geography   24
      The coastal plain   24
      The hill-country of Judah and Samaria   25
      The Negeb   26
      Galilee   26
      The Jordan valley and the Dead Sea   27
      Transjordan   28

3. The historical framework   31

   The origins of Israel   31
   The period of the monarchy (1020–587)   34

The beginnings of the monarchy, from Saul to Solomon
(1020–931)   36
  Saul (c.1020–1000) and Ishbaal (c.1000), kings of Israel   36
  David (c.1005–970), king of Judah, then of Judah
    and Israel   36
  Solomon, king of Judah and Israel (c.970–931)   37
The two divided kingdoms (931–722)   38
  In the North (Israel or Ephraim)   39
  In the South (Judah)   40
The kingdom of Judah after the fall of Samaria (722–587)   40
  Hezekiah (728/727–698)   40
  Manasseh (697–642) and Amon (642–640)   41
  Josiah (640–609)   41
  Jehoiakim (608–598)   41
  Zedekiah (598–587)   42
From the exile to the Roman period (from 587 BC
to AD 135)   42
The time of the exile (from 598–587 to c.525)   43
The Persian period (539–333)   43
  The exiles return to Jerusalem   44
  The rebuilding of the Jerusalem temple (520–515)   44
  The revolt and the destruction of Babylon (482)   45
  Nehemiah's mission (445)   45
  Ezra's mission (398)   45
The Hellenistic period (333–63 BC)   46
  Alexander the Great (333–323)   46
  The Lagids or Ptolemies (323–200)   46
  The Seleucids (200–164)   47
  The Hasmonaeans (164–63)   47
The Roman period (from 63 BC)   48
  Antipater (64–54) and the struggle for the succession
    (43–37)   48
  Herod the Great (37–4 BC)   48
  Archelaus (4 BC–AD 6)   48
  The Roman procurators (6–66)   48
  The First Jewish War (66–70)   49
  Judaea after the destruction of Jerusalem (70–132)   50
  The Second Jewish War (132–135)   50

4. The Book and the books 51

The Hebrew Bible 51
  The Torah or the Pentateuch 52
    The structure of the collection 53
    The question of the 'sources' or 'traditions'
      of the Pentateuch 54
    The classic theory of documents or traditions 57
    How do we see the origin of the Torah today? 58
  The Nebi'im or 'Prophets' 62
  The Kethubim or 'Writings' 65
The Greek Bible (LXX) 65
  Greek text and Hebrew text 67
  The organization of the LXX 67
    The historical books 68
    The poetical and didactic books 68
    The prophetic books 69
    Conclusion 69
The Christian Bible 70
Conclusion 71

5. Foundation stories 74

The 'Book of Origins' (Gen. 1–11) 75
  The biblical narrative 75
  The facts 76
  The interpretation 77
The history of the patriarchs (Gen. 12–50) 79
  The biblical narrative 79
  The facts 80
  The interpretation 81
The history of Moses (Exodus-Deuteronomy) 86
  The biblical narrative 87
  The facts 89
  The interpretation 90
The history of Joshua 93
  The biblical narrative 94
  The facts 94
  The interpretation 95

The history of the judges   97
    The biblical narrative   97
    The facts   97
    The interpretation   98

6. The period of the monarchy   100

The history of Saul and David   100
    The biblical narrative   100
    The facts   102
    The interpretation   102
The history of Solomon   106
    The biblical narrative   106
    The facts   106
    The interpretation   107
The two independent kingdoms   108
    The biblical narrative   108
    The facts   109
    The interpretation   110
Judah, from the destruction of Samaria to the
    destruction of Jerusalem   112
    The biblical narrative   113
    The facts   113
    The interpretation   113
The prophets   114
    The biblical narrative   114
    The facts   118
    The interpretation   121

7. The great trial   124

The Deuteronomistic school   124
    Current hypotheses about the Deuteronomistic school 125
    The theology of the Deuteronomistic school   126
The Priestly school   128

8. **The time of God's silence** 131

Zerubbabel and the second temple 131
  The biblical narrative 132
  The facts 132
    The temple 132
    The festivals 134
    The liturgy of sacrifices 135
    The song of the Psalms 135
  The interpretation 136
    The divine abode 136
    The sacred mountain, centre and microcosm 137
    The place of divine stability 137
Nehemiah and the theology of the 'remnant' 139
  The biblical narrative 139
  The facts 139
  The interpretation 142
    The experience of suffering 142
    The interpretation of this suffering: YHWH remains silent 143
    The reason for YHWH's silence: the sin of his people 144
    The hope of the 'remnant': divine forgiveness and conversion 144
Ezra and the theology of 'YHWH's poor' 145
  The biblical narrative 145
  The facts 146
  The interpretation 148
    The suffering of the 'poor' 149
    The innocence of the 'poor' 149
    The awaited return 150
    The temple, centre of all life 151
    A 'messianic' and hierarchical community 151

9. **The challenge of the new culture** 152

Koheleth or Ecclesiastes 152
Sirach or Ecclesiasticus 155
Daniel 161

The Book of Wisdom   166
Conclusion   168

10. **The Lamb**   171

'According to the scriptures'   173
The scriptures, 'proof' of Jesus?   174
Scripture, the key to understanding Jesus   175
Jesus Christ, the key to understanding scripture   176

Epilogue   179

Answers to questions in the boxes on pp. 56–61   181

Introduction

Moses sent them to spy out the land of Canaan, and said to them,
'Go up into the Negeb over there, and go up into the hill country,
and see what the land is, and whether the people who dwell in it are
strong or weak, whether they are few or many, and whether the
land that they dwell in is good or bad, and whether the cities that
they dwell in are camps or strongholds, and whether the land is rich
or poor, and whether there is wood in it or not. Be of good courage,
and bring some of the fruit of the land.' Now the time was the sea-
son of the first ripe grapes.
So they went up and spied out the land from the wilderness of Zin
to Rehob, near the entrance of Hamat. They went up into the
Negeb, and came to Hebron; and Ahiman, Sheshai and Talmai, the
descendants of Anak, were there . . . And they came to the valley of
Eshcol, and cut down from there a branch with a single cluster of
grapes, and they carried it on a pole between two of them; they
brought also some pomegranates and figs (Num. 13.17–24).

What a discovery! A land 'flowing with milk and honey' and plenty of
fruit to pick! That's the prospect for anyone today who sets out to
explore the biblical countryside. It's a mysterious land, which one
enters somewhat apprehensively. But it's a beautiful, fertile, welcoming land for those who risk the journey, provided that they take their
time and don't get stuck in byways. Taking the plunge is always an
adventure. And the exploration is never finished.

Why read the Bible? How are we to understand it? These are questions not only for Jews and Christians but also for those who do not
belong to any established religion. Contemporary philosophers, writers

and artists derive an important part of their inspiration from the Bible, and the whole of Western culture has deep roots in it. But how do we get into the Bible?

A great book . . .

The Bible is the holy book of Judaism and Christianity (and there are also echoes of it in the Qur'an). It is part of the cultural and spiritual wealth of humanity, like the greatest works of art. It is the most published and most read book in the whole world. Translations have multiplied in every language, and we are seeing a new interest in it not only in Western Christianity but also in more remote areas.

. . . essential to the faith of Christians . . .

The New Testament provides the foundation of faith for Christians, no matter what confession they belong to; it is their foundation document, on which the reflection and life of the church is based. Despite the hesitations expressed in the second century by Marcion (see the last chapter of this book), Christians also consider the books which now constitute their 'Old' or 'First' Testament as their holy scripture. In it they find human testimony to the roots of their faith, which they also welcome as the revelation of God and the testimony of his living Word.

In the Catholic Church, many people remember the time when the laity were advised not to read the First Testament – were even forbidden to do so – and priests did not read it very much. This mistrust goes back to the fifteenth and sixteenth centuries. The first important translation of the First Testament into a modern language was made by the Prague theologian Jan Hus, who was accused of heresy and burned at the stake in 1415; a century later, the great Reformers (Luther and Calvin in particular) circulated the first of the printed translations of the Bible in the vernacular. Moreover they emphasized that the Bible was the sole source of revelation and that it could not be subject to any magisterium. In reaction the Catholic Church forbade the reading of Protestant translations, which for a long time were the only ones which could be read by the majority of people. Today the situation is quite different. Since the beginning of the twentieth century a move-ment of a return to the Bible has developed in Catholic circles; there are excellent translations and innumerable studies, from the simplest to the most learned; the First Testament has been reintroduced into the liturgy and, here and there, into catechesis. All this is encouraged by the church at the highest level; the most important statements are Pope Pius XII's encyclical *Divino afflante Spiritu* (1943), the Vatican II Constitution *Dei Verbum* (1965), and the document by the Pontifical Biblical Commission entitled *The Interpretation of the Bible in the Church* (1993).

. . . but hard to get into

To discover the riches of the Bible it is not enough to open it with good intentions or to declare that it is the 'Word of God'. In practice it poses real difficulties. Here are some of them.

The cultural distance between the world of the Bible and ours is considerable. What flowed from the sources at that time is unknown to us or seems strange. We have to discover another planet. In these conditions, how do we read the Bible without remaining outside the text, like tourists who do not see anything of the real life of the country in which they spend their holidays?

Our civilization favours whatever is practical, rational, efficient. It has little room for symbols. How in this case can we recognize behind the details that these stories are about our lives, too? How can we escape the double trap of an archaeological reading (the text as a witness to a bygone age) and a dogmatic reading (the text as a ready-made truth, which relieves us from reflecting and evades the most urgent challenges of our societies)?

The geographical and historical references escape us. How can we become interested in this figure or that people when we know only names, and have no points of reference?

For Christians, reading the Old Testament comes up against a difficult question: hasn't it been superseded and supplanted by the New Testament? How are we to accept texts which refer to an angry, interventionist God, bound to a single people, when Jesus revealed a God of goodness, whose love is offered to the whole of humankind?

In the Protestant world there is a well-founded tradition of reading the Bible in its two Testaments. Among Catholics, despite the progress mentioned above, almost everything has still to be done. Since the last liturgical reform, one page from the First Testament has been read at mass every Sunday. The progress is obvious! But is it enough to read one page isolated from its context? It has to be added that this reading is often almost incomprehensible, barely integrated into the movement of prayer, and even the homily does not always provide much illumination. In school or parish teaching practices vary. When the Bible is read (and that is quite rare), study of it remains at the anecdotal level. There are few places which give training in really reading it.

As a result of this, for most people – including Christians – the Bible remains a closed and inaccessible book. Those who risk opening it, close it too soon, without having had time to savour its taste.

So?

The Bible is a precious treasure. Reading it can enrich all those who open it, and in particular can nourish the faith and hope of Christians. However, reading it does pose real difficulties, relating not only to the outward form but also to basic questions. We can read the Bible fruitfully only on certain conditions. It is best to have a guide for exploring the exceptionally rich ground of the Bible; those who dispense with one risk being discouraged. The sole aim of this book is to provide a few landmarks, so that exploration can be engaged in without too much difficulty and it is possible really to encounter the heart of the biblical experience. Here are some keys, but they are worthless unless you use them to enter the building and discover its riches. So the important thing is not to read these pages: their sole aim is to make it possible to open the Bible itself, to discover its flavour, and become a reader.

I

How do we read?

What can we expect from reading the Bible? When we open the book, what do we hope, secretly, to find? Some will say, 'The divine Word given to humankind of every age.' Others will say, 'A human word, of its time, fragile and always provisional.' A divine word or a human word? Perhaps we have to use both terms. That, at any rate, is the conviction of the Christian community as expressed by Vatican II *(Dei Verbum* 11). If the Bible is only human, why say that it is so important, when there are plenty of more knowledgeable, more learned, more profound or more attractive books? If it is not a human word, how can we get into it?

The question has a parallel in christology, since the Christian churches confess Jesus Christ as both 'true God and true man'. There are two possible ways of expressing this mystery. One is the way 'from above, downwards': from the start Christ is endowed with the classical attributes of divinity, in particular omniscience. In these conditions how can we still take his human dimension seriously? How can we still say that he truly put on our human condition and made our suffering his own? That is why numerous theologians prefer the way 'from below, upwards', which also follows the fundamental experience of the believer. Jesus appeared to his contemporaries as a human being whose words and behaviour made some wonder, scandalized others, and caused everyone to ask questions. He appeared as an enigma, and everyone asked questions about his identity: could he be a prophet, perhaps *the* Prophet, or even the Messiah? It was only after the experience of Easter, after feeling the presence of the Risen Christ beyond his death on the cross, that the community of the disciples of Jesus came, stammeringly, to understand that the mystery of Jesus surpassed all that had been said previously. Didn't he address God with the familiar word *'abba,* the word used by a human child to its father? Didn't he have an absolutely unique relationship with God? God is always the Other, the one who escapes us, the one who is greater than the images constructed by human beings. But from then on, in order to know God, Christians have looked at the man from Nazareth: through his human choices, his human words, Jesus reveals the face of God. Now it is not necessary to know what in Jesus is 'human' and what is 'divine': his human consistency is our only access to the mystery of his divinity.

It's the same with scripture. To begin by proclaiming the divine origin of the Bible brings with it the risk that its human, earthly dimension, bound up with specific circumstances, can no longer be taken seriously. If, however, readers accept this word as a witness of men and women, a witness rooted in real experiences, they can begin to understand how this same word is addressed to them by God. They must again listen and become involved in a demanding dialogue with the other who is speaking.

The foundation documents

There are two kinds of human words. Often what people call 'words' are no more than chat, meaningless remarks to pass the time. Other words provide more or less important information. But some words deserve this name in a strong sense: they express a real experience; they aim to move the hearer. Testimony is a prototype of this kind of word. The Bible presents itself to its readers as the testimony of a community of believers of former times who, with all the resources at their disposal, have tried to give an account of what has happened to them.

When witnesses speak, they do not seek to communicate words, but what they have seen or see: events. These events are most important for them. If it is true that the Bible is a word of testimony, then it is not enough to study the text for its own sake. The witnesses are writing to share with their readers what they themselves have discovered: the events which have touched them, their questions and their certainties, their desire to be faithful, their faith, their hope. So we mustn't separate the words from the history of which they seek to give an account.

Scripture reports facts. It tells a story, But this is an interpreted story, the meaning of which unfolds step by step. We mustn't imagine a divine revelation flashing out in very distant times, and then a more or less faithful transmission of this. On the contrary, we can speak of a progressive experience: its beginnings are obscure, but little by little it matures towards the full revelation of God. Israel learned to read its history as a history of salvation, in the course of which God educates his people and reveals to them the multiple facets of his mystery.

It is through this long course that God speaks or, more precisely, allows himself to be discovered. The reader today can welcome, in faith, the very Word of God through a thousand human words. Not directly. To neglect the human weight of this word would be the easiest way of misunderstanding it. The authors of the Bible are people who, Jews and Christians say, are 'inspired': they have written in the Spirit of God. This presence of the Spirit must not be limited to the inspiration of the writers as such, far less to certain prestigious authors like Moses, David or the prophets. After all, in many cases the whole believing community has had the experience to which scripture bears witness. It was this community which, in stages, recognized the books of the Bible as sacred and thus formed what we call the 'canon of scripture', handing it on to later generations. Believers can recognize the action of the Spirit in the whole of this process. The human witness of the Bible is one of the main places where the Spirit of God speaks to human beings and puts them on the way.

We still have to ask what is the ultimate purpose of this witness and how far it is true. This truth must not be sought in the scientific realm. The authors of Bible simply accepted the science of their time; for example, they put the hare among the ruminants (Lev. 11.6). Similarly, the Bible is a mine of first-class information about history, but the facts are interpreted, and not everything can be trusted to the same degree. Thus certain parallel accounts contradict each other on various points, and the four Gospels cannot be entirely harmonized. The truth of the Bible must not be put on a theological level either: we do not find in it unified, homogeneous thought, but theologies interacting with one another. So, Vatican II tells us how we must understand this truth:

'The books of Scripture, firmly, faithfully and without error, teach that truth which God, *for the sake of our salvation*, wished to see confided to the sacred Scriptures' (*Dei verbum* 11). The Bible speaks the truth, since it leads readers to God's salvation: it 'does the truth' in them, and orientates them on their true human vocation. It is not surprising that Christ presents himself as 'the way, the truth and the life' (John 14.16).

Listening for the Other

So God speaks in scripture through the testimony of human beings – human beings situated in the context of their time. We will be able to hear the divine voice only if we are attentive to the human voice of the Bible. Besides, how can we claim to be tuning in to the Other *par excellence* if we are incapable of hearing those who are like us?

Thus to read the Bible is to welcome the experience of others than ourselves and what they are seeking to express. This kind of listening is always difficult, since everyone has prejudices: before hearing what the other person is saying, we think that we know what he or she is going to say. To listen properly, we have to accept that other people are different, unexpected. We have to have faith in them: what they say may surprise us, amaze us. This gift of listening to what another person is really saying in depth is rare, all too rare. It requires our entire attention; we have to be available and really open our minds and hearts.

In dialogue, it is never easy to listen to someone else. We think we can hear the other, and yet we are listening to ourselves. However, the person with whom we are talking can react and say, 'You haven't understood me!' When reading the Bible, the difficulty is even greater, for we have to take into account the cultural distances and our prior images of God or faith; moreover, the authors can never contradict us when we have failed to understand them. No one comes to the Bible without prejudices, without a certain idea of the text they are about to read. So there is a real danger that we will find in the Bible only the reflection of our own thought, and will not be listening to the other who is speaking. Our only chance of understanding what God says in the Bible is to silence our prejudices as far as possible and set out really to listen to the word of the other. That is the spiritual attitude *par excellence*, one which is truly open to the action of the Spirit. Spirituality is not a matter of the state of the soul, but rather the welcoming of this Other who will always surprise us. It presupposes that we will really work on ourselves.

How can we protect ourselves against the illusion of understanding, so that we acquire a certain objectivity in reading? The name of this effort is biblical exegesis. This term does not denote a particular method but a series of reading techniques aimed at helping us to listen more closely to the word of the Bible. All these techniques suggest a critical approach. This is not a matter of criticizing the text, as some people suspect, but of criticizing our preconceived ideas, our naiveties, our idols.

So to read is to make sense of the text we have before us or, more precisely, to allow it to become significant for us. One of the most tenacious prejudices is the idea that the text has one well-defined sense that needs to be discovered, over and above the succession of words and phrases. In reality the text does not have one sense; it has several. Similarly, our life does not have one sense that we could define (there can still be some surprises in store for us); we can presume that it has several senses. We shall never have finished understanding the text that we read, any more than we shall have finished understanding our human life. In these conditions we must not try to discover *the* 'good' way of reading the Bible as opposed to all the others, saying that these are bad or wrong. There are several legitimate ways of reading, and that is a good thing. It is true, however, that not all readings are valid: some are richer, more evocative, more attentive to the text or cover more of it. Be this as it may, no one can read without risking interpretation.

We can distinguish two major types of possible readings: one set are concerned to locate the text in its historical context, while the others take the text as it appears in our Bibles, without worrying about its origins. These two approaches, far from being exclusive, are complementary.

Historical readings

Classical exegesis of the kind practised for more than two centuries is also called 'historical criticism': it sets out to discover the message that the author of the text wanted to pass on 'in those days', the intention which inspired him when he wrote. This type of exegesis has serious limitations: it calls for a great deal of preparation and competence which only specialists have; its results always to some degree remain hypothetical; it risks paying attention exclusively to the archaeology of the text, to the detriment of its current meaning. Today everyone agrees that the author's intention does not exhaust the sense of the text. However, that is its initial sense, and to that degree it is has a particular value. That is why classical exegesis continues to be important.

To understand what someone else says presupposes as thorough a knowledge as possible of that person's culture and history. In fact modes of expression vary from one place to another, and from one period to another. If we do not know the rules according to which someone is speaking, we are open to many misunderstandings. That is why for a long time biblical exegesis has been attentive to the question of literary genres. Similarly, knowledge of the historical context in which each redactor is active to a large extent conditions our understanding of his message. Other approaches have progressively completed this form of enquiry. It comprises a number of aspects:

(a) *Textual criticism*: this is concerned to restore the best text possible, on the basis of the major manuscripts (which contain variants) and ancient versions (above all the LXX, or the Greek translation called the Septuagint). We will never get back to the original text, but without a solid textual basis, everything else is built on sand.

(b) *Semantic and linguistic analysis* is aimed at understanding the meaning of words and phrases (grammar, etc.). If the meaning of a little-used word is obscure, recourse is had to analogies with neighbouring Semitic languages (Ugaritic, Accadian, Arabic, and so on).

(c) *Literary criticism* (in the classical sense) sets out to define literary units (or 'pericopes') and check their coherence. Often the exegesis will find indications that the text is composite. In the nineteenth century and for a good part of the twentieth the usual explanation was that the author was using several sources which he had juxtaposed. That, for example, is the classical theory of the formation of the Pentateuch (the first five books of the Bible: Genesis, Exodus, Leviticus, Numbers, Deuteronomy): independent documents from different eras were thought to have been assembled to form the present text. Today, increasingly, this type of explanation has been abandoned in favour of a hypothesis of the literary growth of texts by the phenomenon of 're-reading' or 're-writing'. The ancient text is illuminated by being compared with a new experience (a political event, increased spiritual maturity . . .) and a new redactor copies it again, introducing into it expansions which seem to him appropriate.

(d) *Form criticism and the criticism of literary genres* recognizes 'families' among the mass of texts: several passages present a common literary form (the same structure, the same use of typical expressions), which is the indication of a common literary genre. So narratives (of various kinds, like chronicles and legends) are distinguished from laws, oracles and prophetic sayings (here too we have to distinguish different types), didactic texts, prayers and so on. We do not read parables as we do legislative texts.

(e) *Redaction criticism* tries to reconstruct the history of the text from its first beginnings to its final state, setting out as far as possible to discover the procedures and motivations of the redactors at each stage. For example, a particular narrative or oracle again became relevant when the Jerusalem temple was destroyed and Israel had the bitter experience of a terrible misfortune: at that time the text was rewritten with the addition of new elements. So it will be necessary to distinguish several stages of the text, each of which expresses a specific theology.

This investigation ends up considering the actual text, the only one which appears in the Bible. That leads to so-called 'synchronic' readings.

So-called 'synchronic' readings

For a long time exegesis of a historical kind enjoyed a virtual monopoly. However, from the 1960s and 1970s onwards, attention came to be focussed more on the present text of the Bible, read with the help of methods developed for the study of contemporary texts. A whole series of approaches has been proposed.

(a) *Semiotic analysis* approaches the text from the perspective of structuralism. It is based on three major principles: the principle of immanence (consider all the text, but only the text and not its literary or historical context), and the principle of the structuring of meaning by the relationship between the different elements in the text (oppositions . . .), and finally the principle of the grammar of the text at its different levels.

(b) *Narrative criticism* is concerned with the narratives. It studies the way in which a story is told; in particular it notes the development of the plot, the presentation of the characters and the perspective adopted by the narrator.

(c) *Rhetorical analysis* studies the dynamic of persuasion that the text uses through different stylistic procedures.

(d) *The canonical approach* suggests reading the text in the light of the fact that it is part of the canon of scripture as this is accepted by the believing community; this firmly theological approach begins from the faith of the community and ends with the relevance of the text in the churches today.

It should be added that many contemporary studies are also based on the Jewish and patristic traditions or refer to the human sciences (sociology, cultural anthropology and psychoanalysis). They are no less stimulating.

The work of exegesis is often presented as a dissection of the text, which takes people away from faith rather than nourishing it. This criticism is sometimes well-founded. However, all in all, critical exegesis performs a valuable service for believers, since it is concerned that they should understand their faith. If it is true that exegesis consists in using different methods in order to be able to listen better to the Other who expresses himself through the human witness of the Bible, its approach is eminently spiritual, even if it is rigorous and critical.

Fundamentalism

Fundamentalism should not be confused with traditionalism (Christianity that seeks to be faithful to the tradition, which is too often confused with particular expressions of Catholicism in the nineteenth century) or with integralism (radical and often aggressive conservatism). Fundamentalism came into being in certain Protestant circles at the beginning of the twentieth century; it rejects any critical or figurative approach to the Bible: since the Bible is the word of God, one can only interpret it literally in all its details. For example, it will be explained that the world was indeed created in six days, even if that means saying that modern science is wrong. By its simplistic approach and its absolute affirmations, the fundamentalist reading attracts a large number of people who look for an immediate answer to their questions in the Bible: isolating a phrase is enough for them to to have the illusion of being in possession of 'the truth'. It goes without saying that such a reading, which is particularly valued in groups with a sectarian tendencies, provides only false certainties. The Roman document entitled *The Interpretation of the Bible in the Church* describes it as 'intellectual suicide'.

Making a covenant

Witnesses are not content with informing: if they describe their experiences, it is to evoke a reaction on the part of their audience, to enter into dialogue with them. It is the same with the biblical witness: the Word is given to evoke new words, to lead to a new dynamic in the relationship. The Bible speaks of covenant here. Thus the Bible invites us both to listen respectfully, trustingly, and in an intelligent way and also to make a personal response, on the basis of our own personal and collective experience and our own faith. Such a dialogue between the faith received from the tradition (the biblical Word) and the faith of believers today allows them to nourish themselves and develop: thus we too are able to become witnesses in our turn. That is the conviction of the Christian community: if scripture is not contemporary, if it is not a word which brings life today, it is no longer living scripture, and its reading will only be the memory of a bygone past.

This practice of the reappropriation of the Word is traditional. It led to the very growth of the biblical corpus, from the first narratives and the first oracles to the books which form the canon of scripture today. The traditional Jewish reading of scripture goes in the same direction when it distinguishes four levels of comprehension:

(a) The *peshat* or 'peeling' of scripture according to its literal mean-ing: this is a matter of rediscovering the meaning of the text in its historical context.
(b) The *remez* consists of being guided when reading by associations with more or less similar texts. It is involvement in a vast interplay of allusions or reminiscences. For example, a comparison will be made between the book of Ruth and the story of the secret anoint-ing of David in I Samuel 16, because the two texts tell a story which took place in Bethlehem.
(c) The *derash* or 'quest' describes a freer approach: a search for a deeper, hidden meaning which is sometimes the opposite of the text at the level of the *peshat*. All sorts of techniques are possible, like gematria (a play on the numerical values of letters) or anagrams.
(d) The *sod* or 'secret' is the unfathomable domain. Here readers efface themselves in awe before something that is entirely beyond them.

Traditional Jewish Bible reading is a never-ending quest: one will never be able to discover the final meaning of the text. Above all the practice of *derash* involves reappropriating the text, extending it and relating it to other texts in order to make it meaningful. We also find the same practice of reappropriating scripture behind what have been called the 'spiritual meanings' of the Bible as practised by the church fathers and the Christian writers of the Middle Ages. Each of these is a way of actualizing the first Testament in terms of the faith, love and hope taught by the gospel. Thus the Fathers distinguished four senses of scripture:

(a) The *literal sense* is the one that the reader attributes spontaneously to the text in its supposed historical environment.
(b) The *allegorical sense* is gained in faith: from that perspective all scripture is focussed on the mysteries of Christ and the church, the

---

Midrash and Targum

Scripture is a living text which is not imprisoned in the circumstances of its composition but always remains open to a new sense for those who read it. This process of re-reading or actualization is incarnate in two ancient Jewish practises, the Midrash and the Targum.

The *midrash* (from the root *darash*, 'seek') denotes both a method of interpretation and works composed by this method. Two types can be distinguished. The *midrash halakah* ('way') is interested in moral and legal questions; it offers rules of conduct, laws. In the Bible the writings of the Priestly school follow this line. The *midrash haggadah* ('narrative') extends the biblical texts by telling stories with a generally edifying tone. The books of Ruth and Jonah are biblical examples of this practice.

The Targum is a very free oral translation of scripture into Aramaic. During the Persian period (sixth to fourth centuries BC) the use of Aramaic spread in Israel, to such a degree that Hebrew came to be used only as a sacred language. In the liturgy, scripture was read in Hebrew; then a scribe translated it into Aramaic so that everyone could understand (see Neh. 8–9). While translating, he would allow himself to express his understanding of the text freely. The main Targums, which were fixed in writing towards the beginning of our era, are valuable witnesses to the interpretation of Scripture in the time of Jesus and the growing church.

---

body of Christ. Beyond its literal sense, the text is thought to be open to a second sense, sometimes thought to be deeper. Up to the fourth century a distinction was made only between the literal sense and the 'spiritual' or 'mystical' sense. When people came to talk of the four senses of scripture, in practice allegory was confused with what was called the 'figurative' or 'typological' sense of the texts. For example, the words addressed to the serpent in Gen. 3.15 were read as the 'protevangelium', the first announcement of redemption, with the victory of the descendants of Eve (Jesus Christ or Mary) over the serpent, who represents the Devil.

(c) The *tropological sense* relates to love: every text in scripture can call for some kind of moral conduct. Here it is a matter of action: the characters in the Bible are models to imitate or, quite the reverse, models not to imitate, and their example puts people on their guard against the dangers of misconduct.

(d) The *anagogical sense* corresponds to Christian hope. This time, it
can be said that the biblical text is focussed on the goal to be
achieved, the end of time.

The Fathers themselves and Thomas Aquinas remind us that the literal
or historical sense comes first: the first thing is to understand what the
biblical authors meant to say. The so-called 'spiritual' meanings are
like harmonics evoked by taking into account the unity of the whole
of the Bible. They must not be set over against the literal sense: that
is open to later developments. That means that the same text can
have several meanings; in a way, one can even assert that it takes on
different meanings for each of its readers.

The Bible best read in the church

Exegesis renders an important service, but it cannot claim to be the
only way of reading the Bible. That is not reserved to intellectuals, but
is given as a treasure for all. In fact, several registers of reading have
to be distinguished. Outside the work of professional exegetes there is
the careful study of the text, alone or with others, which calls for
appropriate attention and methods: here joining a Bible study group
and the use of exegetical works is more fruitful than working by
oneself. In the Catholic tradition there is also *lectio divina* or personal
meditation on texts, which has been practised since antiquity, particularly in a monastic context; this meditation results in prayer, but also
in pastoral action. However, the best place for Bible reading is the
church and, as always, the liturgy. Reading scripture is always pre-
scribed for the celebration of the sacraments and is desirable, at least
where there is pastoral opportunity; similarly, the Bible occupies an
essential place in the liturgy of the Hours. However, for the majority
of Christians the Sunday eucharist is the time when they will be
brought into regular contact with the word.

At the eucharist, the ministry of the word precedes and illuminates
the eucharistic action. When the assembly gathers, in fact it begins by
listening to the Bible. In principle three readings are proposed for
Sunday and festivals, even if for pastoral reasons sometimes only two

are kept: usually there is a reading from the first Testament linked to the theme of the Gospel, then a passage from the letters of Paul or another New Testament writing, and finally a passage from the Gospels. Nor should we forget the psalm, which invites us to pray with the words and very movement of the Bible. The homily consists of restating this threefold word as it relates to the present day. The biblical word, situated 'at that time', is always new and always topical; it is fulfilled in the life of the assembled Christian community, notably in its liturgical activity.

This practice of the church presupposes a threefold conviction. First of all, beyond its apparent diversity the Bible forms a profound unity, and thus scripture illuminates scripture. Then this word gives the church, and each Christian, the essentials that they need to live out their faith; it is the living source to which we can always return to draw on. Finally, the Bible is the book of the believing community, before it is a book for individuals: it is first of all in the church, when the community gathers to live out the mystery of the living Christ, that the Word can be welcomed for what it is.

By way of a conclusion

A scene from the Gospel of Luke shows Jesus in action as a reader of the scriptures:

> And he came to Nazareth, where he had been brought up; and he went to the synagogue, as his custom was, on the sabbath day. And he stood up to read; and there was given to him the book of the prophet Isaiah. He unrolled the book and found the place where it was written, 'The spirit of the Lord is upon me . . . ' (Luke 4.16–18).

Here is the reading of the book in the framework of the liturgy, in the presence of the whole believing community. The words chosen by the narrator express in a vivid way the way in which Jesus reads.

(a) The book is *given* to Jesus. In other words, he does not make use of it to deliver his own message but he receives it; later on, he gives it to the attendant (v.20). To read is to receive a word which does not belong to us, and then to pass it on for others to receive in their turn.

(b) Jesus *unrolls* the book, which takes the form of a scroll. The gesture is evocative. One does not read the Bible all at once; one must patiently unroll it and follow the text step by step. It is not enough to take this or that fragment out of context. On the other hand, neither the Bible nor the Gospels can be reduced to an 'essential message' that could be summed up in one or more phrases. Scripture is complex, multiform, and its riches can be received only by patient unrolling.

(c) Finally, Jesus *finds* the passage he is going to read. This finding is not a chance affair, since Jesus has unrolled the book in search of something. However, the verb suggests an unpredictability, as if the reader was ready to be surprised, and did not want everything to be under his control. Reading is not seeking to know: the book will open if we have the desire to find.

(d) Note, further, Jesus' commentary: '*Today* this passage of scripture is fulfilled in your ears' (v.21). If we take the trouble to read, it is not in order to acquire learning, to accumulate knowledge external to ourselves; it is because this word becomes meaningful today, for us and for our world, because it brings life.

The first key to the scriptures is the desire to read, not to gain knowledge but to receive from the Other his word, which can always surprise and amaze us.

2

The geographical framework

The biblical narrative constantly refers to places: landscapes (the wilderness, the lake…), towns and villages, rivers, regions… The story that it tells, which conditions it, is set against a varied background. So to understand the Bible we need to take account both of the map of the area and of the wider map of the ancient Near East. Nowadays these maps are included in the appendices of the better Bibles; it is important to get into the habit of referring to them to locate the sites mentioned in the text.

Geography of the ancient Near East

Israel lived in the world of the Near East, with which it had constant political and cultural relations. Initially it barely differed from the surrounding populations, and only step by step did it begin to stand out by virtue of its way of thinking and living. Even then it remained closely connected with the brilliant civilizations which influenced it.

The ancient Near East is dominated by two main centres of civilization: Mesopotamia, or the land of the two rivers (the Tigris in the east and the Euphrates in the West) which flow into the Persian Gulf, and Egypt, with the Nile Valley and Delta. In the fourth millennium BC the first great societies to have a structure and a system of writing came into being: Sumerian civilization (around the cities of Ur, Larsa, Urik, Lagash, etc., with cuneiform script) and the first empire of the Pharaohs (with hieroglyphs). These two civilizations took various forms over the course of history, but generally speaking they persisted throughout the whole of antiquity: one could say that the whole of the

---

Use the tools in your Bible

The best editions of the Bible contain not only a translation of the text but also a series of tools which help you to read it. For instance, you will find in the *Jerusalem Bible*:

- introductions to major literary complexes like the Pentateuch or to certain books like the Apocalypse; at varying length, these introductions present the text which follows and sum up exegetical research on it, but without going into the details of particular hypotheses;
- references in the margins indicating the most similar texts (the same expression, the same image, the same theme) or quotations in other books of the Bible; some references indicated with a + refer to footnotes which are useful for reading the text;
- footnotes which have various objectives: to explain the textual variants and the choices made by the translator; to present briefly a narrative or a speech; to put the passage in its historical context; to explain a word or a cultural feature; to suggest perspectives from biblical theology;
- a chronological table of the history of the Bible and the ancient Near East;
- the genealogy of the Hasmonaean and Herodian dynasties;
- a table of Near Eastern calendars indicating the Israelite festivals;
- a table of measures and coinages;
- an alphabetical table of the most important notes;
- several maps of the Near East and the region of Syria-Palestine, with two plans of Jerusalem.

The use of these various tools will itself enrich Bible reading considerably.

---

life of the region gravitated around the two poles of Egypt and Mesopotamia. Between the two is the great Arabian desert, which stretches northwards through the plains of Syria. So the two major centres of the 'fertile crescent' could communicate only through the narrow corridor of Syria-Palestine, squeezed between the Mediterranean and the desert. The country of Canaan, occupied by Israel, was in the southern part of this corridor, which was fought over by the great empires. The country was a commercial route, but also the site of numerous battles. This situation conditioned the whole of the history of Israel: a buffer state between the great powers, it was tempted to form an alliance now with one and now with the other, unless it was just a victim of conflicts which were quite beyond it.

Mesopotamia

In Mesopotamia (present-day Iraq), life is conditioned by the rivers. These form immense alluvial plains and sometimes overflow catastrophically. Unified by language (Accadian) and script (cuneiform), Mesopotamia itself has two centres of gravity. The land of Sumer is situated in the southern region, near the estuary of the two rivers. This ancient civilization was supplanted in the third millennium by Semitic populations, which formed the land of Accad (Sippar, Borsippa, Nippur) and then Babylonia (Babylon-Babel). Assyria (Assur, Nuzi, Nineveh) developed in the north. Periodically we see a ferocious struggle for supremacy between these two poles.

Mesopotamian literature is very rich. Several important texts developed in the Sumerian period and then were rewritten in Accadian. We should particularly note some major works which present analogies to the Bible:

(a) The epic of *Atrahasis*, which relates the creation of humankind, charged with working the earth, something that the lower gods no longer wanted to do. However, the human race multiplied to such a degree that the gods, exasperated by the racket, decided to suppress it. Only one man escaped the scourge, but he gave rise to a new humanity, and the problem arose a second time, and then a third. The third scourge was a flood. This very ancient narrative shows significant analogies to the first eleven chapters of Genesis (creation of the first human being, multiplication, flood).

(b) The *Gilgamesh* epic, known at Sumer, in Assyria and Babylon and also in Palestine and among the Hittites. It tells the story of a proud man named Gilgamesh. The gods produced a rival to him, Enkidu, but Enkidu became his friend. However, Enkidu died, and Gilgamesh, who also feared death, left in search of the 'plant of life' which was to bring him immortality. After numerous trials he succeeded in getting hold of the plant, but immediately was robbed of it by a serpent, so he had to accept his mortal condition.

In this text we find a long flood story, several details in which agree with the biblical narrative.

(c) The poem designated by its first words, *Enuma Elish,* i.e. 'When on high . . . ' This text is the great Babylonian creation narrative, which has affinities with Gen. 1. Creation results from a dramatic combat between Marduk, god of Babylon, and Tiamat, the incarnation of evil.

(d) Mesopotamia had an extensive wisdom literature, with proverbs, fables and oracles, and also several texts which describe the human condition in a very sombre light, recalling the book of Job: the Sumerian poem known under the title 'Man and God'; the 'Pessimistic Dialogue'; and the Babylonian poem *Ludlul bel nemeqi,* often known under the title 'The Righteous Sufferer'.

Egypt

The whole life of Egypt depends on the river, even more so than that of Mesopotamia. Once again we can distinguish two regions: Lower Egypt, which corresponds to the Nile Delta, and Upper Egypt, concentrated in the long ribbon of the river valley. On both sides lies the desert, which is almost uninhabited. But where the Nile passes through, life is luxuriant, fed by the floods of the river, which regularly deposits its silt. In periods of crisis the two regions are separate; in times of great success (the Old Empire, from 2635 to 2154; the Middle Empire, from 2030 to 1720; the New Empire, from 1552 to 1070), the Pharaoh reigns over 'the two lands', symbolized by his double crown. Only in the sixteenth century BC did the Egyptians go beyond their natural frontiers to occupy vast regions in Syria and Palestine.

Egyptian religion gave a major place to the sun, first of the gods and guarantor of the world order. In contrast to the Mesopotamian mentality, marked by tragedy, here we find an optimistic view: the gods, who watch over the beneficial deposits of the Nile, are good; after death a new life awaits human beings. Egyptian literature is known in Israel, which is influenced in particular by the wisdom writings, collections of advice intended for senior officials or the king (The Instruction for Ptah-hotep; The Instruction for King Meri-ka-re; The Instruction of Amen-em-opet, etc.). On the other hand, the monotheism of Akenaten in the fifteenth century is only a passing moment which had no future.

The other centres of civilization

The Near East cannot be reduced to these two main poles. In the corridor of Syria-Palestine lies the land of Canaan, which developed a brilliant civilization known today through the archaeological discoveries at Ras Shamra, the ancient kingdom of Ugarit, on the Lebanese coast. Canaanite religion, centred on the divine figures of El (creator god) and above all Baal (god of fertility), was expressed by agricultural feasts which Israel inherited; moreover in the Bible we find numerous images and expressions which come from Canaanite civilization.

Another civilization plays an important role in the ancient Near East: the Hatti or land of the Hittites, which is essentially present-day Turkey. The Hittite empire, Egypt's great rival, disappeared around 1200.

Archaeology and the Bible

Both the region of Syria-Palestine and the neighbouring countries have been the object of increasingly numerous and precise archaeological excavations. The results of this research are of great interest to Bible readers. They give us better knowledge of the civilizations of the Near East from material evidence (architecture, urban culture, utensils, etc.). Some sites contain documents (sometimes even whole libraries), which shed new light not only on the economic, social, cultural and political history of the populations concerned, but also, in more than one case, on their religious life. Archaeologists are still working today on many sites mentioned in the Bible, and this sometimes provides confirmation of the biblical text. However, it is important to be very careful here, as the identification of places remains uncertain. Moreover, material agreement with the biblical narrative does not always prove that the narrative is historically correct; for example, the presence of traces of fire do not indicate who caused it. In other cases, the result of excavations seems to contradict the narrative. Be this as it may, today archaeology is the basis of all historical reconstructions.

To the east and north-east, Mesopotamia is bordered by a vast mountain region (present-day Iran), from which marauding tribes regularly descended. The Persian empire had its centre in this region.

Palestinian geography

The land of Israel is situated in the southern part of the corridor of Syria–Palestine, between the desert and the Mediterranean. The country is not very long: at its greatest extent, from the sources of the Jordan to Eilat, it is around 240 miles as the crow flies, but biblical Israel, 'from Dan to Beersheba', is far smaller (around 150 miles). Several very different regions can be distinguished: the coastal plain; the hill-country of Judah and Samaria with the promontory of Mount Carmel; the Negeb; the Jordan valley and the Dead Sea; Galilee; and the regions of Transjordan.

The coastal plain

A line of dunes and a plain extend all along the Mediterranean coast, briefly interrupted by the promontory of Mount Carmel, near the present-day city of Haifa. So we have to distinguish two quite different zones.

North of Mount Carmel, along the bay of Haifa and up to Rosh Haniqra (the Lebanese frontier), stretches the valley of Zebulon, the width of which varies from between around three to twelve miles. This well-irrigated and fertile plain was formerly inhabited by fishermen and farmers. The tribe of Zebulon is located here.

The plain south of Mount Carmel is more extensive. Very narrow around Carmel, it then forms the Sharon, on average around seven miles wide (and about thirty miles long); then it broadens out, and finally meets up with the border of the Negeb. This fertile region was very important both commercially and strategically, since it was necessary to pass through it to get from Egypt to Mesopotamia or to the land of the Hittites. In the biblical period it was the land of the Philistines, who established five city-states there from around 1200: Ashdod, Ashkelon, Gaza, Ekron and Gath. Up to the year 1000 the

Philistines tried to get out of their natural sphere and to conquer the hill-country; despite some success, they eventually abandoned this plan. However, we need to note that this region was almost never Israelite, at least in antiquity.

The hill-country of Judah and Samaria

Parallel to the Mediterranean, about thirty miles away, is a ridge of hills which, following the summits from south to north, goes through Hebron, Jerusalem, Bethel, Samaria and Shechem. Then the chain curves westwards, meeting the Mediterranean at Mount Carmel. This mountain range forms the heart of the land of Israel. The summits can be as high as 1,500 metres around Hebron and 1,000 metres near Bethel; then they gradually get lower and lower towards the north. Three zones can be distinguished from north to south: the massif of Carmel, the hill-country of Samaria and the hill-country of Judah.

Mount Carmel, which rises to around 580 metres, forms a rocky spur which dominates the Mediterranean and blocks off the coastal plain. Its name means 'orchard', and the mountain has always been a symbol of fertility. It is the scene of one of the exploits of Elijah, who in the ninth century BC massacred four hundred and fifty prophets of Baal there (I Kings 18). To get from the coastal plain to lower Galilee and thus reach Damascus and Mesopotamia it was necessary to go over one of the three passes which cut through the mountain and which are controlled by the citadels of Yoqneam, Megiddo and Yibleam. These strategic places – above all Megiddo, the easiest way through – saw numerous battles: Revelation 16.16 locates the decisive battlefield between God and the forces of evil in Armageddon (an allusion to the 'Mountain of Megiddo').

The hill-country of Samaria – with its extension by Mount Gilboa, further north – was inhabited by the two main tribes of central Palestine: Manasseh to the north and Ephraim to the south. The tribe of Ephraim was itself divided, giving rise to the tribe of Benjamin ('son of the south'). The region seems to have been wooded until around the twelfth century; the valleys become increasingly wide as one goes northwards. Shechem is in the north of the hill-country; until the tenth century it was the symbolic centre of Israel. The great assembly of the tribes after the settlement in the country took place there (Josh. 24). It was there, too, on Mount Gerizim, which dominates the city, that the Samaritans had their temple.

The hill-country of Judah (or Judaea) is where the tribe of this name settled, from Jerusalem to Beersheba. This austere countryside, the centre of which is the city of Hebron, was quite poor. The two sides of the mountain are very different. Eastwards, the slope is gradual, from the zone of the first hills (the region of the Shephelah or 'low country'; the main city is Lachish) to the line of the crests. The hills are separated by valleys of varying width, in which agriculture could develop. By contrast, the eastern side drops steeply towards the Jordan valley and the Dead Sea. The erosion of the soil has led to the disappearance of vegetation and very sparse rainfall: so much so that this area has become a desert. It is the wilderness of Judah, small in area but very inhospitable.

Jerusalem lies at the edge of the hill-country of Judah, or more precisely in the area between the hill-country of Judah and that of Samaria. Around 1000 David made this his personal city (the 'city of David'), the joint capital of the two kingdoms which were placed under his authority.

The Negeb

South of the hill country of Judah, there is a vast desert stretching in a triangle as far as the Gulf of Eilat (or Aqaba). There is little rainfall in this region, but the water from the winter storms can flow over the hard ground and form fierce torrents. In ancient times, water collected in cisterns and the use of dew made scanty cultivation possible here and there. The city of Beersheba, which plays an important role in the story of the patriarchs, lies in the north of the Negeb.

Galilee

Watered by rain and well irrigated, Galilee is the most verdant region of the land. It was always somewhat eccentric, and its traditional name, 'Galilee of the Gentiles' (Isa. 8.23), recalls the motley character of its inhabitants and its openness to the outside world. The Israelite populations who lived there had not been in Egypt: they embraced faith in Yahweh as the result of a revolution against their Canaanite overlords with the help of the tribes of central Palestine, in the eleventh century BC (the battle of Mount Tabor, Judg. 4–5).

We need to distinguish two regions: Upper Galilee, to the north, and Lower Galilee, around Lake Tiberias. As its name indicates, Upper Galilee is a mountainous area, the summits of which are well over 1,000 metres high. In antiquity, it was covered with forests and thus sparsely populated. On the eastern edge was the city of Hazor, which was a Canaanite citadel before it became Israelite.

The region of Lower Galilee comprises above all hills, the highest of which barely reach 600 metres. The most famous of these is Mount Tabor, which stands out in isolation in the plain of Jezreel. This broad plain, very fertile today, was once almost impossible to cross because it was marshy: it forms the frontier with the mountain region of Carmel and Samaria. Almost at the centre of Lower Galilee, in the time of Jesus Nazareth was still a very small village.

The Jordan valley and the Dead Sea

The spectacular depression which crosses the whole land from north to south is an exceptional geological phenomenon. The fault begins between the Lebanon and the Anti-Lebanon, follows the course of the Jordan and the Dead Sea, and then the valley of the Arabah, the gulf of Aqaba (or Eilat) and the Red Sea. It is the deepest valley in the world, the level of the Dead Sea (which is itself around 400 metres deep) being some 400 metres below sea level.

The sources of the Jordan, controlled by the city of Dan, correspond to the northern extremity of Israel. They are dominated by the massif of Mount Hermon, which towers to around 2,814 metres and was always considered a sacred mountain. Going downstream we first get to Lake Huleh, at the centre of a broad marshy valley of the same name, which today has been drained and reclaimed. Then comes Lake Tiberias, also called Lake Gennesaret or the Sea of Galilee. The surface of the lake, which was the vital centre of Jesus' public activity, is already around 210 metres below sea level. Between the lake and the Dead Sea the Jordan flows in the middle of a broad desert plain: there is vegetation only near the water. Since, moreover, the river is in reality only quite a small meandering stream, it is a barrier rather than a line of communication.

The Dead Sea is a great inland lake, around fifty miles long. Its high salinity, which excludes any marine life, can easily be explained: the Jordan and the rivers which flow into the sea have only slight mineral content, but the water which evaporates in an intense heat is pure. The region of Sodom and Gomorrah (see Gen. 18–19) is traditionally put at the south end of the Dead Sea.

South of the Dead Sea, as far as Eilat, the depression is called the Arabah. Here again the landscape is a desert one.

Transjordan

East of the Jordan is a mountainous territory, cut by three deep rifts: the streams of the Yarmuk (which joins the Jordan a little to the south of Lake Tiberias), the Yabbok (cf. the famous episode of Gen. 32.23–33), and finally the Arnon, which flows into the Dead Sea. These rifts mark the natural boundaries of several countries, from north to south: Aram (capital Damascus), Gilead, Ammon (capital Rabbah, present-day Amman) and Moab. The biblical narrative speaks of the occupation of these regions by several Israelite tribes: Machir, Gad, Reuben. In fact it is above all the land of Gilead, control of which was disputed with Aram, which was marked by an Israelite presence; Penuel, on the Yabbok, was even the capital of Israel for a while in the tenth century.

Finally, south-east of the Dead Sea is the land of Edom. The mountain of Edom faces Mount Peleh (Mount Halaq) on the other side of the Arabah. It seems that the primitive history of Esau (identified with Edom) and Jacob (described as *halaq*, clean-shaven) describes the confrontation of the population of these two regions (see Gen. 27). In late biblical literature Edom is the implacable enemy of Jerusalem.

Some symbolic places

As well as places that we can find on the map, in the Bible there is a whole symbolic geography which is just as important. Here are some examples of it:

- The prototype of the *mountain* is Sinai (or Horeb, in Deuteronomy and related literature). That is where earth and heaven meet, the place where God shows himself and makes himself present to people, especially to communicate his will (the Law) to them. That explains why Zion (the temple mount, in Jerusalem) is presented as a mountain which is higher than all the others (Isa. 2.2; Micah 4.1), or even why Jesus delivers his great 'sermon' on the mountain (Matt. 5.1), withdraws to a mountain to pray (e.g. Mark 6.46), and appears transfigured 'on a mountain' (Mark 9.2 and parallels).

- The *wilderness* appears as a test, which is a passage through death. Here the prototype is the forty years wandering of Israel in the time of Moses (read Deut. 8.2–6). It was during the journey through the wilderness, from the land of slavery to the land of promise, that the people encountered their God on Sinai. The same theme of the wilderness as a place of testing appears in connection with Jesus (Luke 4.1–13 and parallels). But the Bible also speaks of a transformation of the wilderness into a good land, with plenty of water: read Ezek. 47, where we see water flowing from the temple (= the Law), to give life to what was the territory of death.

- In the Bible – as in a much wider literature – *the sea* evokes the threat of evil, terror, the forces of death. It is the primitive chaos, older than creation (Gen. 1.2); the coalition of peoples who assail Jerusalem as the centre of the cosmos organized by YHWH (Ps. 46). In the First Testament the sea is tamed, circumscribed within precise limits (see e.g. Job 38.8–11). Similarly, Jesus tamed the storm (Mark 4.35–41 par).

- The *well* or the *spring* gives fresh water which, in contrast to the sea, is a symbol of life. In numerous texts this beneficial water represents the Law, which gives life to the world; see for example the image of the four rivers of paradise (Gen. 2.10–14) or again Ezek. 37, which has already been mentioned above. The book of Proverbs issues an invitation to drink water from one's own well (5.15), i.e. to remain faithful to the Law and to reject foreign wisdoms like that of Hellenism.

- In the Gospels, *the two shores* of Lake Gennesaret (or Tiberias) represent the confrontation of the Jewish and the Gentile worlds. Jesus constantly goes from one shore to the other, and it is when crossing over that he has to face the tempest.

- In contrast to the holy city of Jerusalem, *Galilee* is perceived as a place open to the 'ordinary' world and, notably, to the pagan world: it is 'Galilee of the nations' (Isa. 8.23). By contrast, Jerusalem is the city of the temple, turned towards God but also separated from the world by its ramparts. The 'holy city' is opposed to the profane world, that of everyday life.

3

The historical framework

The Bible relates the history of Israel in ancient times, and it is itself written on the basis of this historical experience. The narratives were written in response to certain vital questions raised in specific circumstances (for example, 'What are we to say about God after such and such a foreign invasion?'), and the prophets pronounced their oracles with a similar concern. It is impossible to understand what the authors wanted to say without at least an approximate understanding of the circumstances in which they spoke. So a knowledge of the history of Israel is of prime importance for any attentive reader of the Bible.

The question raised in this chapter is a very simple one: what happened in Israel between its origins and the New Testament period? The biblical narrative is the prime – and sometimes the only – source for reconstructing this past. It must not be forgotten that this is a partisan account, and therefore biassed! Historians must take account of the literary genres and subject the text, like any other, to historical criticism. They must also take into account, with the same critical care, the facts of archaeology and other written sources. In other words, no one can claim to reconstruct the events objectively; there are lively discussions among specialists even on important points. The account in the following pages will keep to the main lines and suggest a plausible reconstruction of events: however, by its very nature it is open to discussion.

The origins of Israel

The earliest traditions of the Bible do not seem to go back beyond the thirteenth century. These traditions present the ancestors of Israel as semi-nomads, keeping sheep and goats. The countryside is dominated by the Canaanite city-states, under the control of Egypt.

The populations of Palestine at the dawn of the history of Israel

To simplify (for we have to take account of transitional situations), we can distinguish two types of culture: sedentary and semi-nomadic.

Citizens and countryfolk

The sedentary population live in fortified cities and villages, most often in houses made of dried clay. The literary sources from the Late Bronze Age (from around 1600 to 1200) reveal the diversity of this population, the dominant elements in which preserve the memory of an ethnic origin: Hurrians, Hittites, etc. This diversity corresponds to the picture that emerges from the lists of pre-Israelite peoples of Palestine. These include, in addition to the Canaanites, which is a generic name: 'the Kenites, the Kenizzites and the Kadmonites, the Hittites, the Perizzites, the Rephaim, the Amorites, the Girgashites and the Jebusites' (Gen. 15.19–21). Most are of Semitic origin.

Canaanite society in the Bronze Age was characterized by a flowering of urban civilization. The country had numerous fortified cities, above all in the plains and in the Shephelah. The most important of these (Megiddo, Hazor, Gezer and Jerusalem . . .) formed the centres of little independent states, each with a king and a council of 'elders' or 'nobles' at its head. Canaanite society is often compared to feudal society with its strict hierarchy.

The cities controlled the neighbouring countryside, where the majority of the population lived. The countryfolk cultivated fields of cereal crops or vegetables, and also vines and other fruit trees; they reared cattle, but could also have sheep and goats.

Small cattle breeders

The semi-nomads lived in black tents which they could move around. They reared sheep and goats, but could also have cows or beasts of burden (asses and camels); occasionally they cultivated the land. Even if some of them gradually settled – the women did not accompany the men with the flocks to winter pastures – they barely mixed with the countryfolk, though they were in regular contact. They practised seasonal transhumance, spending the winter in the semi-desert steppes like the Negeb, which then had sufficient vegetation, and the summer in the cultivated areas. They had to come to some agreement with the countryfolk, and this could give rise to conflicts. For the nomads, cultivated land is a country where life is easier, 'where milk and honey flow'; this explains the desire to possess their own land (see the promises to the patriarchs) and the tendency to settle down. This process took place in stages and could extend over several generations: it does not mean the infiltration of people from a long way away, but the settlement of peoples who have been nomadic in a region for a long time.

This description is important for understanding the phenomenon of the origin of Israel, since Genesis presents the patriarchs as nomads who move with their flocks from encampment to encampment. These are not the nomads who cross the desert with their camels, but the small cattle breeders, whose life is precisely as described above. It is also the life of the group led by Moses (Ex. 12; 21; 32; 38).

The birth of the people of Israel is linked to the progressive transition of semi-nomads in the region of Palestine to sedentary life, from around 1200. This was a time of great upheavals: the 'Sea People', who came from the north, were establishing themselves on the coasts of Lebanon (Phoenicians) and Palestine (Philistines); Egypt had great difficulty in repelling them and lost control of the region. Suddenly international trade was interrupted, and the inhabitants of the coastal plain and the Shephelah fled the wretchedness and insecurity and took refuge in the hill-country, hitherto inhabited by semi-nomadic shepherds. The shepherds themselves could no longer obtain from the sedentary population the goods that were vital to their survival, and they found themselves forced to clear the forest and turn to agriculture. That, it seems, is how we are to imagine the emergence of a new civilization in the hill-country of Judah and central Palestine (the territories of Ephraim, Manasseh and Benjamin). At all events, the twelfth century saw the rise of a large number of new, Israelite places in these regions. However, the Canaanite city-states continued to be masters of Galilee and the region around Jerusalem.

Around the same time, other semi-nomadic groups came from the borders of Egypt. They were led by a certain Joshua, whose exploits are recounted in the book of that name. They brought to Israel faith in YHWH, the God who freed them from slavery, along with memories of Moses and a stay in the wilderness. Their faith was soon adopted by all the Israelites, who identified with the people freed by YHWH.

This twofold process gradually became consolidated. In the eleventh century the populations of Galilee overthrew their Canaanite overlords, with the help of the tribes from central Palestine and Transjordan. They in turn adopted the faith of YHWH. This gave rise to a more or less loose league of tribes under the leadership of Ephraim and Manasseh (based on the city of Shechem). In this context the 'judges' mentioned in the Bible are local military leaders whose authority does not extend to all the tribes.

The southern tribes (Judah, Simeon and Levi) and related groups (Caleb and Othniel) had no link with those of central Palestine, but they underwent a parallel development. Here again faith in YHWH was handed down by groups who had experienced the adventure of the Exodus, while the different local populations were absorbed by the tribe of Judah: this was originally fixed in the region of Bethlehem, a few miles south of Jerusalem.

The period of the monarchy (1020–587)

The period of the monarchy covers four and half centuries (from around 1020 to 587) and in many respects seems to be the 'classic' period of Israelite history, with the reigns of David and Solomon, the flowering of great prophecy and the production of an important body of literature. It is divided into three parts: the beginnings of the monarchy, before the schism (from around 1020 to 931); the period of the two independent kingdoms of Israel and Judah (from 931 to 722); and finally, after the fall of Samaria, the destiny of the lone kingdom of Judah down to the exile (722–587).

Social organization before the period of the monarchy

Up to around the year 1000 there was no central administration or communal political authority. However, each group was aware of belonging to a larger entity. This solidarity is expressed by the fiction of a genealogy: those who are 'brothers' recognize themselves as sons of a common father. All this forms a system which functions on several levels:

- The first cell of social life is the *family* (*mišpāḥāh*) or house (*bayit*), an extended group of kinsfolk living together under the authority of its head or 'father'; slaves and some strangers could be attached to this group. At all events, it was the father who exercised authority, and this was generally handed down to his oldest son; hence we can understand how important it was for the head of the family to be sure of male descendants (see the story of Abraham) and how there could be a struggle over the birthright (see the story of Esau and Jacob).
- Several families grouped together to form a *clan*. This group was made necessary by the demands of communal security. The solidarity was expressed symbolically by descent from a common ancestor: the same blood unites the members of the clan, who are all 'brothers'.
- Similarly, several clans form a *tribe*, which bears the name of its ancestor. Thus the same people is sometimes called 'Israel' and sometimes the 'sons of Israel'. The clearest example of this system is to be found in the 'table of nations' (Gen. 10), in which the names of the descendants of Noah form the names of peoples: the genealogical tree makes it possible to locate the various bonds which unite them. The same is true of the lists of the sons of Jacob; see in particular Gen. 29–30; 49.1–28; Deut. 33. In the tribe, the authority seems to be held by 'elders'.

In theory the tribe, like the family, is a stable entity, based on bonds of consanguinity. In practice the family is very independent. The tribes are mobile entities which can split (Benjamin was formed from a clan of Ephraim), disappear (like Simeon, absorbed by Judah), or regroup, depending on circumstances.

There was no inter-tribal organization. In case of common danger, 'providential' figures arose to assume temporary leadership.

The beginnings of the monarchy, from Saul to Solomon (1020–931)

Why did Israel give itself a king? The decisive factor was the military pressure exerted by the Ammonites to the east (the victory of Jabesh-gilead, I Sam. 11) and the Philistines in the west (battle of Aphek, I Sam. 4.1–11). To resist this growing pressure it was necessary to unify the tribes under the authority of the king. The first king was Saul.

Saul (c.1020–1000) and Ishbaal (c.1000), kings of Israel

Acclaimed as king by the army after having come to the aid of Jabesh-gilead, which was being besieged by the Ammonites (I Sam. 11), Saul was primarily a military leader. He waged a guerrilla war against the Philistines, whom he managed to contain for around twenty years. However, around 1000 the Philistines annihilated the Israelite forces in the plain of Jezreel, near to Mount Gilboa. Saul and his son Jonathan died in the battle. Ishbaal, another of Saul's sons, succeeded him, but only for a short time.

    The authority of Saul and Ishbaal was exercised only over the tribes of central and northern Palestine and Transjordan.

David (c.1005–970), king of Judah, then of Judah and Israel

In the South it was probably during the time of Saul that David became the first king of Judah. He ruled at Hebron and engaged in war against Israel; after his victory over Ishbaal and Ishbaal's assassination, he put an end to the dynasty of Saul and established himself as ruler of Israel. Then he captured Jerusalem and made it his own city (the 'city of David'), the joint capital of the two kingdoms, which were not fused. David won a decisive victory over the Philistines and then subjugated the Moabites and the Ammonites, thus forming a powerful empire on both sides of the Jordan. A shadow was cast on the second part of David's reign by the revolt of his son Absalom, who seized Jerusalem but was finally killed.

    We can see the flourishing of the first true Israelite literature in this period, a literature of political propaganda intended to show the legitimacy of the power of David (a man from the South) over the ancient

kingdom of Saul (in the North): a 'Saul-David' narrative (from I Sam.
11 to II Sam. 7* – the asterisk indicates that the text as we now have
it also includes elements of another kind), a history of Absalom (II
Sam.13–20*), and the first embryonic narratives about the history of
the origins of the world (Gen. 2–9*), Abraham (Gen. 12–15*), Isaac
(Gen. 26*), Jacob (Gen. 25.33*) and Joseph (Gen. 37–42*).

Solomon, king of Judah and Israel (c.970–931)

With David, the empire of Judah and Israel reached its greatest dimensions; his son Solomon was content to profit from his fathers' conquests, though these had been somewhat depleted by the end of his
reign. Benefitting from a long period of stability, Solomon's empire
was marked by success at an economic and cultural level.

The new ruler imposed a rigorous organization on the empire
formed by David. He surrounded himself with a body of officials
which rapidly formed a class of privileged men, and he opened schools.
Solomon's most important administrative measure related to the kingdom of Israel, which he divided into twelve districts (I Kings 4.7–19).
Each of them, under the authority of a prefect, had to provide pro-
visions for the court for one month in every year. Judah was not
included in the list: this exception is a favour shown by Solomon to his
own tribe. The king also formed a professional army, and established
fortified garrisons on the frontiers and in the main strategic centres
(Hazor, Megiddo, Gezer, etc.). He engaged in intense diplomatic
and commercial activity and implemented a policy of major building
works: as well as fortifying several cities he enlarged Jerusalem, and
there built a new royal palace and the temple. All this effort was to
boost his own prestige; for example he had a harem of 700 wives who
were princesses and 3000 concubines (I Kings 11.3). So in many
respects Solomon's reign was brilliant, to the point of rivalling the
splendour of the greater empires.

Solomon's reign was also marked by intense literary activity; here
too political concerns remained predominant. This time the main
intent was to show the legitimacy of the power of the younger son
of David, since the rules dictated that Adonijah, his older brother,
should have been heir. In fact Solomon gained power through a palace

revolution (I Kings 1–2). This literature shows that in his great freedom YHWH designated for the throne the man of his choice, to whom all had to submit. The 'Jahwistic' narrative of the Pentateuch, which takes up and expands several accounts already written in the time of David, was composed with a focus on this problem. Similarly, a long history of David and the accession of Solomon was composed on the basis of the 'Saul-David' narrative and the story of Absalom (from I Sam. 9 to I Kings 2*).

The two divided kingdoms (931–722)

The empire of Judah and Israel disappeared immediately after the death of Solomon: Israel revolted and chose its own king, while the neighbouring peoples who had been made vassals regained their independence. Only Judah still recognized the authority of the Davidic dynasty. For two centuries the kingdom of Judah (in the South, with its capital Jerusalem) and the kingdom of Ephraim or Israel (in the North, with successive capitals of Shechem, Tirzah and Samaria) lived side by side.

> We should note that the word 'Israel' is ambiguous. At a political level it denotes the northern kingdom. At a religious level, and particularly in the mouth of the prophets, it denotes the whole of the people of YHWH in the two kingdoms, as in Isa 8.14: 'The two houses (dynasties) of Israel'. In numerous passages of the Bible the precise meaning of the word 'Israel' is unclear, since both senses are possible.

The respective situations of the two states were quite different. The North had an extensive territory, well-populated and fertile, but suffered from instability in its dynasties; moreover the neighbouring kingdom of Damascus soon posed a threat. By contrast the South, poor, small and relatively unpopulated, benefitted from the dynastic stability and administration inherited from David and Solomon; more remote from the great empires, it survived its northern neighbour by more than a century and a half.

Despite the divisions and disputes between them, the two states retained the memory of having formed a single people. This feeling was beyond doubt based above all their shared faith in YHWH. Even in the eyes of Judah, YHWH is the 'God of Israel', and the schism is seen as a scandal which tears apart the one people of YHWH.

In the North (Israel or Ephraim)

For want of a complete account, here are the most important reigns:

Jeroboam I (939–909) gained independence for Israel on the death of Solomon. He made Bethel and Dan royal sanctuaries.

Omri (885–874) seized power and founded a new dynasty. He built Samaria (a new and very luxurious capital) and formed political alliances with Tyre and Judah. At the same time the cult of Baal developed as a rival to that of YHWH.

Ahab (874–853), son of Omri, pursued the same policy, but he had to go to war with Aram, which wanted to seize the land of Gilead; at the same time, further east, Assyria became increasingly menacing. The biblical narrative makes Ahab and his Tyrian spouse Jezebel the adversaries of Elijah, defender of the cult of YHWH.

Jehu (841–824) ascended the throne after massacring all Omri's family. He restored the cult of YHWH, which was the only one to gain official recognition.

Jeroboam II (783–743), the last ruler of Jehu's dynasty, reconquered important territories, and the country experienced unprecedented economic prosperity. The social divide between the rich and the wretched ordinary people became dramatic. It is in this context that the preaching of Amos (around 760) and Hosea (slightly later) resounds. The scandalous message of these prophets puts in question traditional religious and social views.

From 745 on, Assyria engaged in a systematic policy of conquest under the leadership of Tiglath-pileser III. In 748, a coalition – of which Israel and Judah formed part – was defeated by the Assyrians. For Israel it was the beginning of the end. In 734 the country was drawn by Aram into the Syro-Ephraimite war against Judah, which appealed to Assyria. The next year, Tiglath-pileser III took Samaria and imposed vassal status on the country. In 722, after a revolt and a long siege, Israel was annexed to the Assyrian empire.

In the South (Judah)

With its small population, and away from the main lines of communication, up to the fall of Samaria the country of Judah did not generally have a particularly brilliant history. Now at war with Israel, now its ally, now its vassal, it had its northern neighbour as its main point of reference.

One reign was an exception, that of Azariah, from 785 to 734, which coincided almost precisely with that of Jeroboam II of Samaria. This was a time of stability and prosperity. The era ended in 734 with the Syro–Ephraimite war. From this period up to 701 we hear the preaching of the prophets Isaiah and Micah.

The kingdom of Judah after the fall of Samaria (722–587)

For a century, Assyria dominated the whole of the Near East; even Egypt was invaded after 671. In this context, Judah saw dark days. A minuscule vassal of Assyria, it first attempted several revolts, and then it was totally subjugated. It was not until the reign of Josiah (640–609) that a national resurrection came, which was to be Judah's swan-song: in 605 the country swung into the orbit of Babylon, and 587 saw the catastrophe of the fall of Jerusalem.

Hezekiah (728/727–698)

The era of Hezekiah corresponds to a series of revolts against Assyria by small vassal states in the region of Syria-Palestine. What camp should it join? The king prudently kept out of the 724–722 revolt and witnessed the end of the neighbouring kingdom of Samaria; a new district was built in Jerusalem to house refugees from the north. However, in 705 Hezekiah himself headed a new revolt: after a siege of Jerusalem, the Assyrian Sennacherib dictated harsh conditions to him (701).

The Bible retains the memory of a religious reform by Hezekiah, the scope of which is much debated. During his reign, however, we do find the preaching of Isaiah and Micah, and we must also reckon with important literary activity (Proverbs, etc.).

Manasseh (697–642) and Amon (642–640)

After the dramatic events of 701, all resistance to Assyria seems to disappear. The long reign of Manasseh coincides with the height of Assyrian power, which dominated unchallenged the whole of the Near East. In these conditions Judah could only remain a subject people, paying tribute and providing troops for the army of Nineveh; in return, Manasseh had restored to him the territories which were cut off from the country under Sennacherib. During this period the cultural and religious influence of Assyria on the country intensified.

Josiah (640–609)

Josiah is the last great king of Jerusalem. He profited from the decline of Assyria – now facing a Babylon whose strength was steadily growing – to declare independence for the country and to recapture some territory of the old kingdom of Israel. Thus he appears as the new David and the new Solomon, and a whole literature celebrates the king as 'Messiah'.

Josiah was the author of a great religious reform, corresponding to the Deuteronomic code (Deut. 12–15). The heart of this reform lay in the closing of all the provincial sanctuaries and the centralization of the cult on Jerusalem. Also at this time, after an apparent silence of some seventy years, we see the reappearance of 'conversion prophets', like Zephaniah and perhaps Jeremiah.

The death of Josiah, who was killed in battle at Megiddo, marked the end of this short period of national independence.

Jehoiakim (608–598)

On the death of Josiah, Judah entered a period of profound crisis. The country was first a vassal of Egypt. From 605 (Nebuchadnezzar's victory at Carchemish) it came under the domination of Babylon, but Jehoiakim rebelled in 601. In 598 Nebuchadnezzar besieged Jerusalem, which was soon captured, and the king Jehoiakim was assassinated. Jehoiachin, who succeeded him, was deported to Babylon along with the nobility, the soldiers and men capable of manufacturing arms. These dramatic events were to mark for ever the memory of Israel, which lost the illusion of being always protected by its God. The prophet Ezekiel was almost certainly among those deported. However, it was another prophet, Jeremiah, who was in the forefront of events in Jerusalem from the death of Josiah to the drama of 587.

Zedekiah (598–587)

Set on the throne of Jerusalem by Nebuchadnezzar and initially subject to Babylon, Zedekiah revolted in 588. The city was again put under siege, a merciless one. In July 587 Jerusalem was captured. The ramparts were dismantled, the temple was burned down, the monarchy was abolished and there was a new deportation of the elite to Babylon. However, important groups fled to neighbouring countries, notably Egypt, taking Jeremiah with them. The drama of 586 marks the end of an era: not only was the country from then on put under a foreign governor, but above all the natural disaster raised immense questions about the goodness and justice of YHWH.

From the exile to the Roman period
(from 587 BC to AD 135)

The events of 598 and 587 ushered in a period of profound crisis, which was particularly keen during the great Babylonian exile. However, it would be wrong to think that the return of the exiles allowed the people to restore their former situation or regain its serenity: the wound opened up in the sixth century never completely healed, and the people were afflicted with new misfortunes (foreign domination, division within the Jewish people itself, persecutions, Diaspora . . .). It was during this long and sorry period that faith in YHWH gradually matured, while hope for the breaking in of his kingdom increased. A phenomenon which proved important for the history of Judaism developed during the dramatic events of the sixth century: the Diaspora. From now on the people of Israel no longer coincided with its land: forcibly deported or escaping violence, important groups established themselves for long centuries not only in Babylonia but also in Egypt, and doubtless elsewhere.

The time of the exile (from 598–587 to c.525)

The destruction of Jerusalem was a drama for all; not only was the country ravaged by war and its population dispersed, but there was no longer any temple or king. These events caused an unprecedented religious crisis: YHWH seemed to have rejected his people. From now on it was divided into three groups: those who had fled, those who had remained, and those who had been deported.

Those who fled to neighbouring countries, above all to Egypt, formed numerous communities which spread further.

The situation of the few people who remained in the land was a deplorable one. Among them was a group which did important theological and literary work, the 'Deuteronomistic school', heirs of the great prophets. This group responded to the challenge of faith by emphasizing, within the framework of a covenant theology, that Israel was to blame for its fate. Once trust in YHWH had returned, this group envisaged a new and happy future for Israel. It edited or re-edited with supplements all the religious literature at its disposal: the Pentateuch (Genesis, Exodus, Leviticus, Numbers, Deuteronomy), the 'Deuteronomistic history' (Joshua, Judges, I and II Samuel, I and II Kings) and the prophetic books (Isaiah, Jeremiah, Amos, etc.).

Those who had been deported to Babylon, who included Ezekiel, organized themselves under the authority of the priests, and little by little developed an interesting society. Circumcision was practised and the sabbath was observed, as marks of the bond between YHWH and his people.

After the death of Nebuchadnezzar (562), the Assyrian empire declined, while the Medes and the Persians united under the authority of Cyrus. He seized Asia Minor and then attacked Babylon itself, which fell like a ripe fruit (539).

The Persian period (539–333)

The Persian empire of the Achaemenids, which dominated the Near East for two centuries, covered an immense territory – from the Indus to the Mediterranean. Judah represented only a minuscule part of it. The Achaemenids adopted a policy of religious toleration and encouraged local religions, including that of the Jews. They showed the same spirit in administrative and cultural matters. So it was that the major languages spoken in the empire were recognized by the administration: for relations with Egypt and Transeuphratene (the region of Syria-Palestine), the language was imperial Aramaic, close to Hebrew and used since the Assyrian period for commercial matters. Initially an official language, Aramaic spread to become the usual idiom of Palestinian Jews; some passages of the Bible are written in this language (Ezra 4.8–6.18; 7.12–26; Dan. 2.4–7.28). Parallel to this, the use of Hebrew was increasingly limited to the liturgy.

On the whole the two centuries of the Persian empire were less eventful than the preceding period, even if the Achaemenids had to repress several revolts or engage in frontier wars (notably against the Greeks and the Egyptians). This long period of relative peace allowed the development of trade. For the Israelites, the Persian period was marked by the extension of the Diaspora, but also by conflicts between different groups, reflected in a vast literary productivity. However, historians are handicapped by the small number of points of reference for both the chronology and the conflicting parties.

The exiles return to Jerusalem

Whether or not the 'Edict of Cyrus' mentioned by Ezra 1 is historical, the Persian regime did allow those who had been deported to return to their country of origin. However, many remained in Babylonia, and it was those with the greatest religious motivation (the 'Zionists') who returned to Jerusalem. There was marked tension between those who had remained in the land and the Zionists, who presented themselves as the only true Israelites.

Between 540 and 530, almost certainly at Jerusalem (and not in Babylon, as is often said), an anonymous prophet known as 'Deutero-Isaiah' engaged in preaching; his oracles have been preserved in Isa. 40–55*.

The rebuilding of the Jerusalem temple (520–515)

Encouraged by the preaching of Zechariah and Haggai, the governor Zerubbabel rebuilt the temple. Since the governor belonged to the ancient Davidic royal family, some groups saw hope of a restoration of the monarchy, but this was only a flash in the pan.

The revolt and the destruction of Babylon (482)

Having been spared under Cyrus, Babylon was destroyed in 482 after a revolt. The symbolic capital of paganism (the 'tower of Babel'), it had destroyed Jerusalem and deported its inhabitants. So its fall was seen in Israel as a sign of the end of the pagan world. The books of Isaiah, Jeremiah, Ezekiel and Zephaniah were reorganized on the basis of this conviction: from now on the oracles on the nations formed the centre of these works, between the announcements of misfortune (relating to the past) and the perspectives of the triumph of Zion.

It was beyond doubt around the same time that an anonymous priestly redactor, heir of the reflection that had matured among those exiled to Babylon, re-edited the Pentateuch with a number of supplements.

Nehemiah's mission (445)

In the middle of the fifth century, Jerusalem had an insecure existence and was unable to defend itself. Nehemiah, governor of Judah, undertook to restore Zion: in 445 he rebuilt the walls and repopulated the city with a population made up exclusively of Zionists. It was almost certainly around this time that the spirituality of the 'remnant of Israel' came into being. It is expressed in an abundant literature (the first edition of Job, Psalms, a new edition of the prophetic books, etc.).

Ezra's mission (398)

In 398, Egypt rebelled and became threatening. To ensure the loyalty of Jerusalem, which was on the frontier, Artaxerxes granted it major favours: the community of Zion was reinforced by new emigrants from Babylon and treasures were given to the temple. Above all, the governor Ezra was able to enact for the whole of the Jewish world a law recognized by the Persian authority; this was the Pentateuch, which received its first redaction. This law corresponded to a new religious reform, the essential feature of which was a ban on mixed marriages.

Indubitably Ezra's work coincides with the triumph of the radical tendency in the Jerusalem community over the face of the more flexible tendency which could appeal to Nehemiah. There was an increasingly lively opposition between the 'just' and the 'impious', and this radicalism is expressed in a vast literature in which there is a spirituality of the 'poor of YHWH' (numerous psalms, a new edition of the book of Job, etc.).

The Hellenistic period (333–63 BC)

Lasting for two and a half centuries, the Hellenistic period can be divided into four parts: the reign of Alexander (333–323), that of the Lagids or Ptolemies (323–200), that of the Seleucids (200–164), and finally the Maccabean and Hasmonaean period.

Alexander the Great (333–323)

Having brought all the Greeks together, Alexander victoriously confronted the Persian empire. He seized the region of Palestine in 333 and authorized the Samaritans to build their temple on Mount Gerizim. Above all, Alexander's victory opened the gates to Hellenistic culture, which was soon to submerge the whole of the Near East.

The Lagids or Ptolemies (323–200)

On the death of Alexander in 323, his generals disputed over his heritage (the war of the Diadochi, which lasted until 281). Judaea was conquered by the Lagids or Ptolemies, the Hellenized rulers of Egypt. It benefitted from a status of cultural and religious autonomy, but gradually the influence of Hellenism came to be felt.

Towards the middle of the third century, an anonymous author wrote the book Koheleth (Ecclesiastes), which is a severe critique of traditional Jewish thought. At the same time we see the rise of the Jewish communities of Egypt (Alexandria), which set about translating the holy books into Greek (the Septuagint or LXX).

The Seleucids (200–164)

In 200, Antiochus III of Syria defeated Ptolemy V and seized Judaea, which obtained major favours. An increasingly important section of the population of Jerusalem, particularly the intellectuals, went over to Hellenism; in reaction an important anti-Hellenistic literature was written (Sirach = Ecclesiasticus, Tobit, Nehemiah, some psalms, the final redaction of Job and Proverbs, etc.).

Antiochus IV (175–164) intensified the Hellenization of the country, and the situation became increasingly tense. In 167 the conflict came to a head, and the practice of Judaism was forbidden on pain of death, while the Jerusalem temple was dedicated to Zeus. The blood of the martyrs flowed. While many people hid, or gave in to the situation, two Jewish groups engaged in resistance: the priestly family of the Hasmonaeans (a political project) and Hassidism (a religious project). In this context, we see the flowering of the first apocalyptic literature, particularly the book of Daniel.

The Hasmonaeans (164–63)

In 164, Jerusalem was recaptured by the rebels led by Judas Maccabaeus, and the temple was purified. However, this event, which left a great mark on the faith of pious Jews, was only an episode in a war which went on for more than twenty years. Judas Maccabaeus was killed in 160, and his sons succeeded him (the Hasmonaean dynasty). Judaea experienced a century of independence, but was disturbed by incessant conflicts.

In 152, Jonathan was consecrated high priest, and this brought about a division among the pious Jews between Sadducees (who criticized him for not being of the Zadokite line) and Pharisees (who accepted his priesthood as provisional).

The books of Maccabees were composed under John Hyrcanus (134–105). At the end of his reign the ruling power became reconciled with the Sadducees; this resulted in the secession of the Essenes, who rejected this treachery. The Hasmonaeans gradually expanded their territory, but only to sink into extreme violence. Thus Alexander Jannaeus (104–76) executed 800 Pharisees who opposed his politics, and the civil war which followed claimed at least 50,000 victims.

The Roman period (from 63 BC)

On the death of Salome Alexandra (in 67), there were two rival claimants for power: both appealed to the Roman Pompey, who had just conquered Syria. Roman domination forms the epilogue to the ancient history of Israel.

Antipater (63–43) and the struggle for the succession (43–37)

In 63, Pompey captured Jerusalem and gave power to Antipater, an Idumaean who was not a Jew. The country was shaken by several revolts. On the death of Antipater, several claimants were engaged in a merciless struggle from which Herod, Antipater's son, finally emerged victorious.

Herod the Great (37–4 BC)

Herod administered the country as a Hellenistic monarch, a faithful ally of the Romans. He was a violent and cruel man, who readily resorted to assassination and subjected the country to intolerable levels of taxation. He extended his power to both sides of the Jordan, forming a considerable kingdom, and implemented a policy of great building works: the construction of fortresses (Herodion and Massada, but also the enlargement of the temple and the beautification of Jerusalem). It was in Herod's reign, almost certainly around the year 6 BC (scholars were wrong in their calculations when establishing the Christian era) that Jesus was born, in utter obscurity.

Archelaus (4 BC–AD 6)

On the death of Herod the country was divided. Herod Antipas was given Galilee and Archelaus received Judaea. He bloodily repressed several revolts, but was soon deposed by the Romans because the population were so enraged at his political tyranny.

The Roman procurators (6–66)

From now on, Judaea and Samaria were administered by a Roman procurator, whose residence was at Caesarea, by the sea. The ministry and death of Jesus are to be put in the procuratorship of Pontius Pilate.

From 41 to 44, the sequence of procurators was interrupted by the happy but ephemeral reign of Herod Agrippa. Then the situation deteriorated, and the Romans had to face increasingly numerous attempts at revolt, buoyed up by a lively religious hope.

The first Jewish War (66–70)

The agitation deteriorated into a real war. The Zealots (a radical movement which grew out of the Pharisaic party) headed a great revolt which seized the whole of Palestine. The insurrection, which for a moment seemed victorious, was repressed by Vespasian and then by his son Titus. The war ended in a blood-bath: after a dramatic siege Jerusalem was razed to the ground and the temple burned down. The Christian community of the city took refuge in Transjordan, just in time.

A 'sacred history'?

The Bible relates a history of salvation which extends from the creation to the end of time, passing through the events of the history of Israel. This sense of history is one of the most amazing characteristics of the Bible: there is no history worth mentioning in the majority of other religions, but rather the eternal return of the inaugural actions of the gods and the unfolding of their immutable decisions.

Scripture knows sacred times: the great religious festivals (the feasts of Unleavened Bread and Passover, the feast of Pentecost, the feast of Booths or Tabernacles) when people went in pilgrimage to the temple, and the weekly sabbath. These feasts form a cycle which begins again each year and re-enacts the events at the foundation of Israel's faith: the exodus from Egypt, the gift of the Law on Mount Sinai, the time in the wilderness, the creation. But it is above all in political and social events that the Bible recognizes the action of YHWH: the history of salvation does not differ from history pure and simple. It is a matter of perspective: where some people see only coincidences or the interplay of political forces, others discern – on another level – the mysterious presence of God.

Judaea after the destruction of Jerusalem (70–132)

After these events, Judaea became a separate Roman province. The Jewish world, terribly shaken, reorganized itself in line with the Pharisaic movement (at the academy of Jabneh or Jamnia, inspired by Johanan ben Zakkai).

In 115 there was a new revolt by the Jews of Egypt and elsewhere, which was put down with harsh repression.

The Second Jewish War (132–135).

A last revolt, led by Simon ben Kosiba (Bar Kokhba) and Rabbi Akiba, ended with a Roman victory. The Romans destroyed Jerusalem and built a new city (Aelia Capitolina) in its place, which Jews were forbidden to enter. Judaism reorganized itself in Galilee and in the Diaspora.

4

The Book and the books

The Bible presents itself to us as the Book, the unique Word. It has to be taken as a whole. At the same time, we cannot fail to recognize an immense diversity. History signifies succession and thus multiplicity. There is also a multiplicity of literary genres: poems, narratives which may or not be edifying, collections of laws, etc. Oppositions begin in the first chapters of Genesis, with the juxtaposition of the two creation narratives, one beginning from the abysses of the waters (Gen. 1) and the other from dry land (Gen. 2). So the Book is a library comprising a number of books. These are organized into two different series in the Hebrew Bible and the Greek Bible (the Septuagint), not to forget the New Testament

The Hebrew Bible

The Hebrew Bible is composed of twenty-four books written in Hebrew or, marginally, in Aramaic (parts of the books of Daniel and Ezra). There are three groups of varying importance: the Torah (= 'the Law', or, better, 'the Teaching'), the Nebi'im (= 'the Prophets') and the Kethubim (= 'the Writings'). So great is the difference in status between these groups that there is no special word to denote 'the Bible'; for example there are several mentions in the Gospels of 'the Law and the Prophets'. Present-day Judaism has constructed an acronym comprising the first letters of the three titles: Tenak or Tanak. The Torah, which was the first to be regarded as a 'holy book', is *the* revealed word; the Nebi'im give a first commentary, composed by the prophets, and the Kethubim a further commentary. They are followed by the Mishnah, which collects in writing the oral teaching of the law from the second century BC. The Mishnah is in turn the nucleus of the Talmud, which gathers together the teachings of the ancient rabbis. So there is a gradation in the authority of these books, which also corresponds to their relative antiquity.

Books, chapters and verses

In the Hebrew Bible each book is denoted by its first word, and over the centuries there has been no other division, except for pauses which are not numbered. It goes without saying that it was not easy to find a precise phrase! That is why a system of references was progressively invented.

- In the Greek Bible, the books were given names corresponding to their content: Genesis or Book of beginnings, Exodus or Book of the departure from Egypt, etc.
- The division into books and chapters was introduced by Stephen Langton in AD 1226.
- In 1561 the printer Robert Estienne refined this system by dividing the chapters into verses, each of which corresponded roughly to a phrase. This division is practical, since it makes it easy to find one's way around the Bible. However, it must be remembered that it does not always correspond to the primary meaning of the text.

The Torah or the Pentateuch

The Torah comprises the first five books of the Bible: Genesis, Exodus, Leviticus, Numbers and Deuteronomy. This work has also been given the name 'Pentateuch', i.e. 'five scrolls'. In it we find a long narrative which runs from the creation of the world to the death of Moses, interspersed with legislative sections. Thus the teaching contains both narratives and laws. We shall examine in turn the structure of the collection, the question of its sources or traditions, and finally the way in which we can now imagine its origin.

The structure of the collection

We can see agreements between Genesis and Deuteronomy, and between Exodus and the book of Numbers.

Genesis relates the history of origins (from the creation to the tower of Babel) and of the patriarchs (Abraham, Isaac, Jacob and Joseph). Deuteronomy is essentially a long speech by Moses , who encourages Israel to be faithful to the Law on the point of entering the promised land. At first sight the two books have nothing in common. However, the endings match. Genesis ends with the blessing of the twelve sons of Jacob (ch. 29), and then with the deaths of Jacob and Joseph (ch. 50). Similarly, the ending of Deuteronomy contains the blessing of the twelve tribes (the same names as those of the sons of Jacob, ch. 33) and then the death of Moses (ch. 34). We should note the importance of the themes of blessing and cursing both in Genesis (3.14, 17; 4.11; 8.21; 9.25–26; 12.2–3, etc.) and in Deuteronomy (chs. 27–28).

The parallel between Exodus and Numbers is striking. Each of these books contains two parts, hinging on the arrival (Ex. 19.1–2) and departure (Num. 10.11–36) from Sinai. The same motifs recur in the journey from Egypt (Ex. 1–18) and along the route which leads from Sinai to the frontiers of the Promised Land (Num. 11–36): the journey through the wilderness, the murmuring, the manna and the quails, the battles against pagan peoples, the water flowing from the rock.

At the centre is the book of Leviticus, dominated by the contrast between clean and unclean, sacred and profane. Here again it is possible to note a concentric arrangement: at the extremes we find on the one hand details of the sacrifices and the priests (chs. 1–10) and on the other the 'Holiness Code' (chs. 17–26 with an appendix in ch. 27). We should remember that sacrifice consists in conveying an offering from the earthly world to that of God, and that the function of the priest is to bring about this transfer. The concept of 'holiness' must be understood in its primary sense of separation: it involves living apart from the profane world, like God. At the centre of this construction we find regulations about clean and unclean animals, the sexual uncleannesses of women and men, and leprosy, the uncleanness *par excellence* (chs. 11–16). So we can construct the following table:

(a) Genesis	(book of curses and blessings)
(b) Exodus	1–18: the journey towards Sinai 19–40: the Law of YHWH on Sinai
(c) Leviticus	1–10: the sacrifices and the priests 11–16: *laws about cleanness and uncleanness* 17–26: the Holiness Code
(b') Numbers	1–10: various regulations on Sinai 11–34: the journey from Sinai
(a') Deuteronomy	(book of curses and blessings)

This construction, which puts the Sinai event at its centre (from Ex. 19 to Num. 10), emphasizing the laws on cleanness and uncleanness, can only be explained as a deliberate choice. Note that the promises of the gift of the land, which take up a great deal of room in Genesis and Exodus, do not end in their fulfilment: it is in the book of Joshua that Israel crosses the frontier and takes possession of the land. Thus the Torah holds out a great hope which it does not fulfil: the book calls for a new word, and for a long time some of the most famous scholars have thought that originally the work comprised not only the first five books but also the book of Joshua. The present break comes either too late (Deuteronomy is the beginning of a narrative which goes as far as the books of Kings) or too early (the promises appeal to the book of Joshua for their fulfilment). This can only be explained by a desire to put the book of Leviticus, with the problems of clean and unclean, at the centre of the perspective.

The question of the 'sources' or 'traditions' of the Pentateuch

Over the centuries, rabbis, church fathers and theologians have scrutinized the text of the Bible, offering a reading which is often very rich. This has made a substantial contribution to the reflection and life of believers. The Bible was *the* 'book of faith', a faith which it nourished and of which it was the primary source. Accepted as the word of God both in the church and in the Jewish world, the first Testament has been studied with great care and subtlety, but without raising today's critical questions, since these arise from reason and not from faith. In this context no one thought of challenging the unanimous tradition which made Moses the human author of the Pentateuch, with the

Clean and unclean, the sacred and the profane

These notions play a tremendous role, not only in the Bible but also in the majority of the religious traditions of the world, and they form a system.

- The *sacred* (or the holy) is a category close to that of taboo: it is the prime quality of the divine as a separate and terrifying reality, which human beings cannot approach without dying. The moral acceptance of the idea of holiness is secondary to awe at the deity. The profane world is of little importance in the face of the sacred powers, on which it is entirely dependent.
- The notion of *cleanness* applies to objects that are pure, homogeneous, without any mixture. Thus animals which fall between two categories are the ones that are judged unclean and so cannot be eaten; for example, aquatic creatures which have neither scales nor fins are not 'real' fish and are unclean (Lev. 11.9–12). Uncleanness – of which the corpse is the prototype – is transmitted by contact.

In the strictest sense, God alone is holy and pure; the temple is the holy place, in which his presence dwells; and the festivals are holy days, consecrated to worship of him. To receive from him the powers of life without which nothing can exist, intermediaries are needed – in particular the priests, who can go into the most sacred areas of the temple. So there are degrees of sacrality, as of cleanness. All this forms a complex system. In the New Testament the distinction between clean and unclean is still mentioned here and there, but only to make it a simple metaphor of moral life (Mark 7).

possible exception of its last verses (Deut. 34.5–12); moreover this 'Mosaic authenticity' was maintained all the more when it seemed to be the guarantee of the divine origin of the book, which was put in question by some Gnostic circles and other Jewish and Christian heretics, and then by learned Muslims.

However, after the Middle Ages, and even more from the eighteenth century on, anachronisms and contradictions were noted, and then a whole series of other literary phenomena, which soon made it necessary to question the Mosaic authenticity of the Torah. Here are the main observations; and then the classical theory which has long been established.

Careful attention to the text has progressively brought a whole series of phenomena to light. Here are some of the most significant.

From this point on, a number of boxes offer an interactive approach, to be used by both individual readers and groups; you will find some brief answers outlined at the end of the book. Later, the boxes will offer a way of reading many of the most significant passages in the Old Testament.

(a) Above all in Genesis, some episodes appear two or even three times with more or less important variants. These are called doublets.

As an example compare Gen. 12.10–20; Gen. 20; Gen. 26.1–11.

- What points do the narratives have in common?
- What are the essential differences?
- How do you explain these observations?

(b) From the eighteenth century on, it was noted that some texts speak of God using the tetragrammaton YHWH (יהוה), the proper name of the God of Israel, while others use Elohim (*'elohim*), a term usually translated 'God'.

The tetragrammaton is rendered in different ways in modern Bibles. The Jerusalem Bible retains the classical usage 'Yahweh', thus following one of the possible pronunciations of the word; in fact this pronunciation is dubious, and several recent studies show that 'Yaho' or 'Yahu' is to be preferred. Moreover Judaism thinks that pronunciation of the Name must be avoided, since there is a risk of being disrespectful. That is why other Bibles render the tetragrammaton by 'the Lord'. That, in fact, is how YHWH should be read aloud.

This phenomenon is particularly interesting when it affects two texts which seem to be repetitions (doublets), but each time with a different divine name; it underlies the classical distinction between 'Yahwistic' texts (indicated by J) and 'Elohistic' texts (indicated by E). In fact the problem is more complicated, since 'Elohim' can be used as a substantive ('the deity'), and we also find composite expressions like 'YHWH your God'.

As an example read Gen. 6.5–8 and Gen. 6.9–13.

- Compare the two narratives, paying particular attention to the divine names.

(c) What is true of the divine names can be extended to other areas. Sometimes the parallel texts use a different vocabulary or phraseology. So we can recognize characteristic turns of phrase from Priestly circles (*miškān*, 'tent-sanctuary'; *'ēdāh*, liturgical assembly', etc.). These differences also relate to certain proper names.

(d) The text also often includes elements which seem to be contradictory. Certainly there are cases where what seems to us to be a contradiction is not really one: it may be a narrative artifice, and this warns us to be careful. On the other hand we can sometimes see breaks in the narrative, as if an alien element were suddenly interrupting it.

As an example read Ex. 6–7.
- Where do we find the divine answer to the question which Moses asks in 6.12?
- Compare this with Ex. 4.

This list could be continued: the same narrative sometimes seems to seek to reply to two different questions; we find different religious, moral, political, legal and social conceptions, etc. What are we to make of all these observations? They would seem incompatible with the tradition that attributes the whole of the Torah to Moses. In fact they can only be explained by quite a complex history of the text.

The classic theory of documents or traditions

The discovery of doublets and the differentiated use of divine names in the eighteenth century produced a first theory: Moses was the author of the Pentateuch, but he used pre-existing documents. This hypothesis proved inadequate, and various theories of increasing complexity were proposed: these were the documentary hypothesis (the collection of independent sources by one or more redactors), the fragmentary hypothesis (an amalgam of a mass of independent units), and the complementary hypothesis (a great, original narrative completed and revised over the course of history).

In 1878, Julius Wellhausen wrote *Die Composition des Hexateuchs und der historische Bücher des Alten Testaments*. This work sets out the documentary theory in its most classic form. Here are the main outlines:

- In the period before the monarchy, oral traditions formed on the basis of tribal memories and rites.
- In the ninth century two important documents were composed: the Book of the Covenant' (Ex. 20.23–23.19, referred to as B), which crystallizes the legislative traditions of the sanctuary of Bethel, and the 'Yahwistic document' (referred to as J), which takes up certain narrative traditions from the South; scholars later than Wellhausen put J in the time of Solomon.
- An 'Elohistic document' (referred to as E) was written in the first half of the eighth century, in the northern kingdom, under the influence of the prophets.
- After the fall of Samaria in 722 the refugees from the North brought the E document to Jerusalem; J and E were combined in a single work by a Judaean redactor called the 'Jehovist' (referred to as R^{JE}).
- In 622, Josiah published the 'Book of the Law', i.e. the central part of Deuteronomy.
- During the Babylonian exile, a group of priests formed the basis of the 'Priestly Document' (referred to as P), bringing together a number of writings including the 'Holiness Code' (Lev. 12–26, referred to as H). This document was to be enriched in the Persian period by a series of supplements (referred to as P^S).
- Finally, around 400 a redactor (referred to as R) brought together the texts JE, D and P, taking P as the overall framework.

Wellhausen's theory is bound up with the mentality of his time (evolutionary thought, German romanticism and mechanistic scientism). With some corrections (like the importance of oral tradition), for a century it served as a point of reference in all critical exegesis.

How do we see the origin of the Torah today?

The documentary hypothesis established itself as a kind of dogma recognized by all, including Catholic exegetes, after the liberating encyclical *Divino afflante spiritu* of 1943. This unanimity fell to pieces around 1975, when numerous works showed the fragility of Wellhausen's construction. For example, it was noted that the prophets of the period of the monarchy do not know the majority of the narratives in the Pentateuch; many of the texts catalogued as J – and thought to go back to the tenth century – show marked analogies with the writings of the Deuteronomic school, which is much later. Coupled with a new view of Israelite origins, these discoveries plunged the classical theory into a state of profound crisis. Today the debate on the formation of the Pentateuch is in full swing, with no view generally accepted.

Since it is impossible to outline the different theories here, I shall content myself with putting forward a hypothesis which takes as much account as possible of a careful examination of the text and Israelite history as it is known today.

(a) The earliest narratives, which use even earlier oral traditions, were set down in writing in the time of David with a political purpose: to show the legitimacy of the power of the king not only over Judah but also over the tribes of the North (the old kingdom of Saul). So an embryonic account of the beginnings (Gen. 1–11*) was set down in writing with a history of the migration of Abraham (Gen. 12–15*) and still primitive stories of Isaac (Gen. 26*), Jacob (Gen. 25–33*) and Joseph (Gen. 37–50*). The earliest account of the exodus from Egypt could be dated to the same period (Ex. 1–15*).

As an example read Gen. 37.3–4, 12–14, 18, 25b-28, 39.1–42.6.
(The text contains later elements and goes at least as far as ch. 46.)

- With what symbolic places are Joseph on the one hand and his brothers on the other associated?
- What could that mean for a reader in the time of David?

(b) Around 950, a redactor at Solomon's court brought together the short narratives from the Davidic period and other traditional narratives to write a consecutive history (document J). Once again, the author's purpose was political: to establish the legitimacy of Solomon, who seized power when in principle it should have gone to his older brother Adonijah (see I Kings 1 and 2). This explains the recurrent motif of the divine choice of the younger son, while the older son is rejected (Cain and Abel, Ishmael and Isaac, Esau and Jacob, the sons of Israel and Joseph, Zerah and Peres, Manasseh and Ephraim) and also the motif of the massacre of the firstborn sons (Ex. 12.29). This narrative began from the creation of human beings (Gen. 2) and extended as far as the journey into the wilderness (Ex. 17). We find material in the same vein in the books of Judges (the call of Gideon, ch. 6; the birth of Samson, chapter 13) and Samuel (the history of the rivalry between Saul and David, the history of the succession to the throne of David); so it is possible that the document in fact extends to I Kings 2.

As an example read Gen. 4.1–5, 8–10, 12b, 16a.

• What is the relationship between the two brothers before the murder?
• And after the murder?

(c) This long narrative J was completed, between 750 and 587, with a set of material of an 'Elohistic' type (E). As well as using the divine name Elohim, these additions have in common a moral reading which goes along with a theology of retribution. This theology emphasizes the quality of the human response to divine appeals and not the gratuitous nature of the divine interventions; it does not appear in Israel before the preaching of Amos around 760. The E texts present the patriarchs and Moses as models for behaviour, while the J narratives were not afraid to present Abraham and Sarah as violent or liars, Jacob as a thief, and so on. The good conduct of the heroes is also faithfulness to the will of God, in particular expressed in the primitive Decalogue (Ex. 20*). There was probably never an E document as such.

As an example read Gen. 21.8–21 and compare it with Gen. 16 J.

• How do you interpret the similarities and the differences?

(d) The next step is that of the Deuteronomistic re-readings (Dtr) at the time of the exile, almost certainly in Palestine. We need to recall the state of mind of the population after the dramas of 598 and 587: the experience of misfortune put in question belief in

YHWH as a God attached to his people. The writers of the Deuteronomistic school, spiritual heirs of the great prophets – Jeremiah in particular – tried to restore to Israel confidence in its God. To this end they edited or re-edited the religious literature of Israel known in their time, notably the old J narrative in its Elohistic version, with widespread additions. This immense work extended over several decades and comprised three or four successive redactions.

As an example read Gen. 18.16–19.28.

• How could this narrative, which includes some older elements, have been understood immediately after the great danger which befell Jerusalem?

(e) Then came the Priestly redaction (P), which stemmed from priests who had returned from Babylon. It integrated reflection that had matured in the trials of the exile and contact with Babylonian literature. Although there is dispute over the question, the existence of an independent P document is improbable; the P texts must almost certainly be seen as a series of additions to the 'textual basis' inherited from the Deuteronomists. In any case, the present text of the Pentateuch is largely structured by the Priestly contribution. P seems to have been writing in the first part of the Persian period, at a moment of disillusionment after the euphoric return of those who had been deported: they had hoped so much that Israel would regain its independence and the prestige of the time of David and Solomon, but despite the rebuilding of the temple, nothing had happened! In this context, P rewrites the Pentateuch to give hope to a discouraged people: behind the appearances there is a marvellous order of the world; nothing escapes it and God is its author.

As an example read Gen. 1.1–2.3.

What images of God, the world and human beings are expressed here?

(f) The final redaction of the Pentateuch (R), is the work of Ezra's scribes, shortly after 400. The emperor Artaxerxes made a request to Ezra, who 'set his heart to study the law of the Lord, and to do it, and to teach his statutes and ordinances in Israel' (Ezra 7.10). Ezra left Babylon with a royal edict, commissioning the governor to apply the Law of his God in Judah and Jerusalem. From now on this Torah would be considered as the 'king's law' for all Israelites in the region of Syria-Palestine (Transeuphratene): not only those who gathered at the Jerusalem temple but also all the others. R conceived his work as a support for the great religious reform introduced by Ezra, the main element of which was the dissolution of marriages between 'true' Israelites and foreign women (Ezra 9.1–10; cf. Gen. 25.23; 26.34–35; 27.46; 28.1–9; 34; 35.5*; Num. 25.6–18). That is why he cut the book at the end of Deuteronomy and put Leviticus at its centre, incorporating into it the 'Holiness Code' (Lev. 17–26). This brought into play the opposition between clean and unclean, linked to the ban on mixed marriages. The same author introduced a large number of ritual prescriptions.

As an example read Num. 25.6–18.

The promulgation of Ezra's Torah as the official law recognized by the Persian authorities marked a decisive stage in the formation of the canon. For a long time the texts which later formed the Pentateuch were authoritative; that is why they were commented on and supplemented at every important stage in the life of Israel. But now the Torah formed a work of such authority that no one was allowed to touch it further: from now on the commentaries would be external to it.

The Nebi'im or 'Prophets'

The Hebrew Bible distinguishes two sets of prophetic books, the 'former prophets' and the 'latter prophets'; both are presented as the first authorized interpreters of the Torah, those who made a specific application of it through the history of Israel up to the time of Malachi (fifth century?) This reading has left its mark on the text, since it is as it were framed by two invitations to remain faithful to the Torah in Josh. 1.6–9 and Mal. 3.22–23.

A number symbolism

Certain numbers in the Bible have been given a symbolic value, to which the Priestly school was particularly sensitive. We should especially note:

- 1: Relates to God. YHWH is the only God, to the exclusion of all others; he is also one, unified, homogeneous as opposed to the multiplicity of the world. Whatever is one and homogeneous is clean; whatever is multiple is unclean;
- 2: The figure of human beings, marked by the division of the sexes; if God is one, the human being is always duality or multiplicity;
- 3: The figure of heaven, or more precisely of verticality (heaven – earth – the underworld);
- 4: The figure of the earth or horizontality (the four winds, which correspond to our four points of the compass);
- 5: The five books of the Torah;
- 7: Totality (heaven/verticality + earth/horizontality) and thus perfection; it is also the figure of the sabbath; multiples of 7 are also important (especially 70);
- 8: In the New Testament, the eighth day is that of the resurrection, the new world inaugurated in Jesus Christ;
- 10: The Decalogue and, by extension, the Law;
- 12: Again totality (the twelve months of the year; 3×4), the twelve tribes of Israel; the multitude of the church is represented in the Apocalypse by the figure 144,000 ($12 \times 12 \times 1000$);
- 40: A generation, the period of testing in the wilderness;
- 666: The number of the Beast (cf. Rev. 13.18).

Judaism developed a whole system of speculation on numbers (gematria), in particular using the totals of the values of letters in a word.

The *former prophets* correspond to a series of four historical books which today bear the very strong stamp of their Deuteronomistic redaction: Joshua, Judges, Samuel and Kings. Originally this long narrative, which extends from the death of Moses to the national catastrophe of 587, formed a sequel to what has become the Pentateuch. These books are put among the prophets because they contain the history of a certain number of prophetic figures like Samuel, Nathan, Elijah, Elisha and Isaiah; similarly Joshua, the judges and the kings are endowed with a certain number of prophetic features (see e.g. II Sam. 23.1–7). The final redaction of this group seems to have been contemporaneous to that of the Pentateuch (around 400).

The *latter prophets* also form four books: Isaiah, Jeremiah, Ezekiel and the book of the twelve 'Minor Prophets' (Hosea, Joel, Amos, Obadiah, Jonah, Micah, Nahum, Habakkuk, Zephaniah, Haggai, Zechariah and Malachi). Each of these collections in fact contains elements from different periods. Usually the starting point is the preaching of a particular prophet. The oracles, initially intended for oral communication, were then set down in writing either by the prophet himself (in exceptional cases) or by disciples. The book thus formed has been edited several times, each time with more or less important supplements. This work seems to extend down to around 200, to the Hellenistic period. From this moment, holy scripture comprises 'the Law and the Prophets'; this second element was envisaged as having been derived from the first.

We should note the diversity of the phenomenon of prophecy and the books which bear witness to it. Initially prophecy is a somewhat marginal phenomenon, on the verge of the paranormal (visions, predictions, phenomena of hysteria). At a second stage the prophets become figures linked to the throne and to the temple, where they exercise an official function; some of these prophets are men of stature, like Nathan or Elisha. Parallel to this, from the middle of the eighth century, we see the rise of some individuals who proclaim oracles in quite a different style, emphasizing the responsibility of the rulers of Israel and announcing terrible disasters: these are the 'conversion prophets'. The most important of them are Amos, Hosea, Isaiah and Micah (in the eighth century), and then Zephaniah, Jeremiah and Ezekiel (around 600). There are also the 'optimistic prophets' at the beginning of the Persian period, who were doubtless the heirs of the official prophecy of the time of the monarchy (Haggai, Zechariah, Deutero-Isaiah etc.). Towards the middle of the Persian period, almost certainly in the fifth century, the phenomenon of prophecy disappeared. This disappearance is bound up with a profound change in Judaism, which increasingly became a 'religion of the book': the whole of the divine revelation is given in the Torah, which must be constantly examined; so the scribe replaces the prophet. However, the prophetic function was prolonged in a new way by the prayer of the psalms, 'new prophecy' of the community.

The Kethubim or 'Writings'

The 'Writings' constitute a third somewhat heterogeneous list comprising the Psalms, the book of Job, Proverbs, Ruth, the Song of Songs, Koheleth (or Ecclesiastes), Lamentations, the book of Esther, Daniel, Ezra, Nehemiah and finally the two books of Chronicles. Here we find a collection of liturgical songs, wisdom books, poetic works and narratives, not to mention the book of Daniel, which can be considered 'prophetic' or 'apocalyptic'. Once again the whole is placed under the sign of the Torah. Thus the Psalter opens with a 'psalm of the Law' (Ps. 1); to live the Law is also to practise wisdom (see Deut. 4.6–8).

The group of the Kethubim contains very ancient material, in particular in the Psalter and in the book of Proverbs, but also much later texts, the latest of which seem to have been composed in the second or even in the first century BC. This third set of books was accepted as holy scripture only towards the end of the first century AD, when Judaism, weakened by the tragic outcome of the first Jewish War, was laying the foundations of its renewal (the academy of Jamnia).

The Greek Bible (LXX)

The Hebrew Bible is not the only Jewish Bible. In antiquity, Greek translations of the Bible appeared, for the use of the numerous flourishing Greek-speaking Jewish communities spread around the Mediterranean basin. The most important of these translations is the so-called 'Septuagint' (LXX). According to the Letter of Aristeas (written between 96 and 93 BCE), seventy-two (or seventy) scholars isolated from one another simultaneously translated the Torah in seventy-two (or seventy) days. All ended up with the same Greek text. Whatever we make of the legend, the LXX was written in Alexandria, from the middle of the third century on; this enormous labour was the work of several authors and extended over a long period. It is impor-

---

The text of the Hebrew Bible

We no longer have the original text of the Bible, but only copies of copies, of copies. Besides, do we have to speak of an 'original text'? As we have seen, the book has undergone a long history, and several variants may have been circulating in parallel. In any case, the manuscripts – papyri and parchments – had only a limited life, so it is not surprising that the oldest manuscript of the Bible (the Aleph codex) only goes back to the tenth century of our era. Hence the fear that successive copyists had significantly modified the text.

However, we now know that this was not the case; they were scrupulously faithful to the text that they had received. In 1947, by chance jars were discovered at Qumran, in the wilderness of Judaea, not far from the Dead Sea, containing texts from antiquity. These included a complete scroll of Isaiah and various fragments of other biblical books. They are the famous 'Dead Sea Scrolls'; they have shown us an aspect of Palestinian Judaism around the time of Jesus which was hitherto almost unknown. What interests us here is that generally the manuscripts have the same text as the mediaeval parchments. So the latter prove trustworthy, at least in essentials. In detail the manuscripts offer a large number of variants. The edition used by specialists today is the *Biblia Hebraica Stuttgartensia*, published in Stuttgart in 1977. It contains the 'Massoretic text' (MT), i.e. the Hebrew text established by Jewish scholars in the Middle Ages, who made the Hebrew easier to read by adding points or signs indicating vowels. This edition, based on the Aleph codex, contains an important critical apparatus, in particular including the main manuscript variants and notable differences from the ancient translations.

---

tant to emphasize that for several centuries the Greek Bible was the holy scripture of numerous Jewish communities; thus it was on the basis of the LXX that Philo of Alexandria, a famous Jewish thinker of the first century of our era, composed his works.

The study of the LXX today occupies the efforts of numerous exegetes, both Jewish and Christian. And with good reason: the Greek text is valuable for establishing the original Hebrew (the work of textual criticism), but also, and above all, it represents a 'different' Bible organized on different principles, and it is in this form that the first Testament became the Hebrew Bible.

Greek text and Hebrew text

All the books of the Hebrew Bible have their equivalent in the LXX. Often the two texts are close and the translation is literal; so recourse to the LXX is interesting when choosing between variants in the Hebrew text. There are other cases where the two texts differ quite significantly. Generally speaking, the Massoretic text (MT) has material over and above the LXX. Did the translator compress a text that he thought was too long? There is debate on the question. However, in more than one case (I Sam. 17–18, the book of Jeremiah), the best studies show that on the contrary the translator has used an original Hebrew text shorter than MT; it is therefore the MT that includes additions. Moreover, sometimes the LXX corresponds in its differences from the MT with certain fragments found at Qumran. Elsewhere the translators have emphasized certain aspects of the text like messianism or the universalism of salvation.

We must reckon that the LXX has a history: it was increasingly corrected to bring it into line with the Hebrew text. Systematic revisions – think of our new translations – were undertaken in the Jewish milieu: these are above all the Bibles of Aquila, Theodotion and Symmachus, all three of which go back to the second century of our era. This work was particularly motivated by the need to respond to Christian apologetic based on the LXX text. Moreover Judaism abandoned the LXX, preferring Aquila, based more closely on the Hebrew Bible. The LXX remained in use among Christians, who produced new editions. Here mention should be made of the vast work of Origen of Alexandria (died after 251), who published a Bible with no less than six parallel texts (the Hexapla). Another important edition is that of Lucian of Antioch (died 311–312), which seems to preserve a very old form of the LXX.

The organization of the LXX

The Greek Bible includes a series of books which do not appear in the Hebrew Bible. They are given a special status: the Catholic tradition speaks of 'deutero-canonical' books (= belonging to a 'second list' of the canon); since the nineteenth century Protestants have regarded them as 'apocryphal' and include them in their editions of the Bible only as an appendix, if at all. On the other hand, there are supplements to several works which appear in the Hebrew Bible (e.g. Daniel). Moreover the order is different: works are grouped by content. Again it has to be explained that this order is not constant in the earliest manuscripts. This phenomenon is linked to the size of the manuscripts, which were initially papyrus scrolls of a limited capacity. Then came the codex (an arrangement like that of our modern books) from the second century AD; from the fourth century, the general use of parchment made it possible to produce volumes including the whole Bible. The order of most current Bibles in English in fact follows that of the Latin Vulgate, itself largely inspired by the way in which Codex Vaticanus and Codex Sinaiticus are arranged, which are LXX manuscripts generally dated to the fifth century.

The historical books

This first part brings together the Pentateuch (= the Torah of the Hebrew Bible) and the 'Former Prophets', to which are joined other books relating the history of Israel: Genesis, Exodus, Leviticus, Numbers, Deuteronomy, Joshua, Judges, Ruth, I–IV Kingdoms (= I–II Samuel and I–II Kings in the Hebrew Bible), Paralipomena (= I and II Chronicles), Ezra-Nehemiah, Tobit, Judith, Esther and I and II Maccabees. Note the logical displacement of the book of Ruth, which relates the history of David's ancestors. Note also that the ancient manuscripts put the books of Ezra-Nehemiah (separated in our editions of the Bible) and Maccabees in very different places, like the group of edifying narratives (Tobit, Judith and Esther). The Greek book of Esther is very different from its namesake in Hebrew. I Maccabees, Tobit and Judith are translations into Hebrew, while II Maccabees was originally written in Greek.

The poetical and didactic books

This second group is put after the prophetic books in some ancient manuscripts. It essentially comprises works belonging to the Kethubim: Job, Psalms, Proverbs, Ecclesiastes (or Koheleth), the Song of Songs, the book of Wisdom, Ecclesiasticus (or Sirach). This last work was written in Hebrew, but the academy of Jamnia did not keep it as part of the Jewish canon of the scripture and it has only come down to us in its Greek version. However, in 1896, the greater part of the Hebrew text was discovered in the Geniza (a place where old manuscripts were stored) of the old synagogue in Cairo; since then other fragments have come to light. The book of Wisdom, on the other hand, is purely a product of the Greek-speaking Jewish community in Alexandria.

The prophetic books

This third group corresponds to the 'latter prophets' of the Hebrew Bible, to which are added other books. So we have Isaiah, Jeremiah, Lamentations, Baruch, Daniel and then the twelve Minor Prophets. Note that the book of Daniel belonged to the 'Writings'; its presence among the prophets corresponds to a characteristic interpretation of the work . . . and of prophecy conceived of as the announcement of events to come; the Greek edition contains important supplements (the song of Azariah, the stories of Susanna and Bel and the Dragon). To the book of Jeremiah are added writings close to the prophet: Lamentations, which is traditionally attributed to him, and the book of Baruch, his secretary; to this must be added the 'Letter of Jeremiah', sometimes included in the book of Baruch.

Conclusion

It emerges from all this that the LXX is not a simple translation of the Hebrew Bible; it is *another* Bible, constructed on different principles. Note an important fact: the Torah has lost its privileged status, to be encompassed in a vaster whole. Over and above variations in the order of books, the principle of a hierarchy between the Torah, the Nebi'im and the Kethubim has been abandoned; from now on we have a single Bible in a logical order. In practice this Bible was to become the first Testament of the Christian world.

It has to be added that each language has its genius, and each translation is also an interpretation. Thus the theology of the LXX, marked by Greek culture and its philosophical vocabulary, will necessarily be different – at least on some points – from that of the Hebrew Bible.

The Christian Bible

In origin the Septuagint is a Jewish book, like the Hebrew Bible. It then became the Bible of Christians (as such, or in its primitive Latin translation, the Vetus Latina), who later added to it the books of the New Testament. After St Jerome (fourth century) and despite long resistance, it was the Latin Vulgate, translated direct from the Hebrew but also including the books of the Greek Bible, which became established throughout the Western Church. After, the attempt made by Jan Hus, who was condemned to the stake in 1415, it was not until the sixteenth century that Bibles appeared in languages other than Latin.

Materially, the Christian First Testament corresponds to the Jewish Tenak. However, we have to understand that the addition of the New Testament modifies its balance. From now on the collection is no longer dominated by the Torah, but by the Gospel. The result is a new understanding of the whole book, and everything converges on a new summit. We should not make the mistake of isolating a few passages said to be 'messianic' and asserting that they proclaim Christ: it is the whole first Testament as such which is affected by the change of perspective.

Let's take a single example: the approach to the Torah. In the Jewish perspective it forms a coherent whole, the centre of which corresponds to Leviticus and the symbolism of clean and unclean. Now we read in the Gospel that Jesus touches a leper, thus crossing the frontier between the two worlds – in the name of God (Mark 1.41) – and when Jesus speaks of the categories clean and unclean, it is to shift the meaning to moral ground (Matt. 15.1–20; Mark 7.1–23). The Gospel reading does not make Leviticus completely irrelevant, as one might believe, but it does force us to make shifts. Moreover this change has to be put against a wider background. The Pentateuch includes both narratives and laws. The Jewish reading favours the legislative element, which dominates the whole of the central part of the collection; emphasizing this feature, we could say that the narratives are a framework and an illustration for the Law. Christians, who do not isolate the Pentateuch, make it the first element in a narrative which extends up to Jesus. Logically it is the narrative element which attracts more attention, whereas the Law is overshadowed, with the notable exception of the Decalogue. The great figures of the narrative (Adam, Noah, Abraham, Jacob, Moses . . .) appear as men who in a way precede and announce Jesus: Leviticus, on the other hand, is largely ignored.

Conclusion

Here, in tabular form, is the order of the books in the Hebrew Bible and the LXX. We note shifts of category, indicating a different way of conceiving of scripture.

Hebrew Bible	LXX and Vulgate
Torah	**Historical books**
	(a) Pentateuch
Genesis	Genesis
Exodus	Exodus
Leviticus	Leviticus
Numbers	Numbers
Deuteronomy	Deuteronomy
Nebi'iim	
(a) Former prophets	*(b) Other historical books*
Joshua	Joshua
Judges	Judges
I and II Samuel	Ruth
I and II Kings	I and II Samuel
	I and II Kings
Latter prophets	I and II Chronicles
Isaiah	Ezra
Jeremiah	Nehemiah
Ezekiel	Tobit
(Hosea, Joel, Amos, Obadiah, Jonah,	Judith
Micah, Nahum, Habakkuk, Zephaniah,	Esther
Haggai, Zechariah and Malachi)	I and II Maccabees

Kethubim	**Poetic and didactic books**
Psalms	Job
Job	Psalms
Proverbs	Proverbs
Ruth	Koheleth
Song of Songs	Song of Songs
Koheleth	Wisdom
Lamentations	Sirach
Esther	
Daniel	*Prophets*
Ezra	
Nehemiah	Isaiah
I and II Chronicles	Jeremiah
	Lamentations
	Baruch
	Ezekiel
	Daniel
	The twelve 'Minor Prophets'
	(Hosea, Joel, Amos, Obadiah, Jonah, Micah, Nahum, Habakkuk, Zephaniah, Haggai, Zechariah and Malachi)

In the Christian Bible this double list is completed by the books of the New Testament

The Gospels	Matthew
	Mark
	Luke
	John
The Acts	Acts of the Apostles
The letters of Paul	Romans
	I and II Corinthians
	Galatians

	Ephesians
	Philippians
	Colossians
	I and II Timothy
	Titus
	Philemon
An anonymous letter	Hebrews
Other letters	James
	I and II Peter
	I, II, III John
	Jude
Apocalypse	The Book of Revelation
	(The Apocalypse)

5

Foundation stories

Some narratives have a special status because they provide the group which hands them on with its foundation. We may call these 'myths'. Not in the trivial sense of a made-up story, but in the strong sense of an inaugural narrative which in a way concentrates the awareness of the group. Such a story always speaks of beginnings. Even when it is relating historical memories, the aim of this story – or at any rate the sole aim of this story – is not to preserve the memory of events. What happened 'at the beginning' represents what the group wants to be: its basic experience, its secret hope. So the past is as it were transfigured, loaded with all the desires of the group, but also with its experience. Stories of this kind, which in fact express a common plan or what one could call a 'philosophy of existence', certainly occur among all peoples, and the Bible contains them too. We can put in this category the creation narratives and, more broadly, the 'Book of Origins' (Gen. 1–11), which tells of the beginnings of the world and humankind, and also the long narrative of the origins of Israel, from the patriarchs (Gen. 12–50) to the history of the judges, not to mention the adventures of Moses and Joshua. This is a vast fresco which runs from the beginnings of the world to the eve of the period of the monarchy. For at this moment we are crossing a threshold: contemporary witnesses are beginning to relate events. In other words, we are entering history as such.

We shall be going through all this, step by step. Each time we shall proceed in three stages. First we shall look at the text in the Bible; then we shall seek to discover what really happened; finally, we shall see how the biblical authors interpret the facts. To understand the following pages you need to have grasped what has been said in the previous

chapters about the history of Israel and the formation of the Pentateuch.

The 'Book of Origins' (Gen. 1–11)

The narratives in Genesis 1–11 are among the best-known pages in the
Bible. Everyone knows the stories about the creation, Adam and Eve,
the flood, and the Tower of Babel. They are part of our culture. Again
we need to get beyond the anecdotes to discover their importance and
depth.

The biblical narrative

Genesis 1–11 comprises a series of narratives which sketch the history
of humankind from its creation to the eve of the call of Abraham: the
account of creation (1.1–2.3), the story of Adam and Eve (2.4–3.24),
the story of Cain and Abel (4.1–16), the story of the flood (6.1–9.17),
of the drunkenness of Noah (9.18–29), and finally of the tower of
Babel (11.1–9).

There is a traditional commentary on this text. To begin with, God
created a perfect world; this world was broken by human sin, which
became deeper and deeper until the moment when YHWH took a new
initiative with the call of Abraham. In that respect Gen. 1–11 would
be the history of decadence under the sign of the curse (3.14, 17; 4.11,
etc.), while Gen.12 would mark the beginning of the history of salvation under the sign of the blessing (12.2–3, etc.). This is only a partial
reading. Not only does the narrative itself speak of a new beginning
with the flood (8.15–9.17), but it takes place under the sign of the
initial blessing of humankind: 'God blessed them and said to them:
"Be fruitful and multiply, fill the earth and have dominion over it"'
(1.28). Despite sin, this blessing – which is the gift of life – is realized
in the growth of humankind expressed by the genealogies of the sons
of Cain and Abel (4.17–26), patriarchs from before the flood (5) and
patriarchs after the flood (11.10–26). Certainly the vital force of
humankind is presented as a progressive regression: the first patriarchs
lived for more than 700 years (except for Enoch, who was transported

to heaven at the age of 365: 5.22–23); after Noah, the life-span diminishes, reaching only around 200 years for the direct ancestors of Abraham, who himself lived 165 years (Gen. 25.7). However, the divine blessing continues to be given to humankind throughout its history. We can read Gen. 1–11 in a descending line, but it is equally possible to read it in an ascending line. Thus the episode of the tower of Babel can be understood as a catastrophe (the confusion of languages) or as decisive progress (the wealth of cultures, the extension of humankind, which from now on occupies the whole earth).

Read Gen. 1.1–11.26.

The facts

It can be said quite clearly that none of the narratives in Gen. 1–11 corresponds to precise historical facts in the past. Neither the history of Adam nor that of Cain nor that of the flood are based on any kind of memory. Besides, the authors of these texts had no intention of writing a historical account. And the reading of their work as an account of the events of a distant past is quite late. Certainly the tower of Babel existed: Babel is the Hebrew name for Babylon, and the tower in question is E.TEMEN.AN.KI, the 'House of the Foundation of Heaven and Earth', an immense ziggurat (stepped temple) built by Nebuchadnezzar I (1123–1101). This ziggurat seems never to have been completed, and the enormous ruin must have been impressive. But even in the case of Gen. 11.1–9 we must not assume historical facts corresponding to the biblical account.

So two questions are inevitable: why were Gen. 1–11 written and how can we affirm that this text is true? The answer to the first question is inevitably complex: like the rest of the Pentateuch, the opening chapters of Genesis have undergone a long literary history (cf. above 52–62). Doubtless the first redactor was inspired by the Sumerian myth of Atrahasis (see 21 above), which already reported the creation of human beings, their multiplication and their destruction by the flood, with the rescue of a survivor. The biblical narrative is gradually filled out from this starting point. It is written because what it says is true, but this is an essential truth which is not that of historical reminiscence. That brings us to the question of the meaning – or better the meanings – of the text.

The interpretation

In the case of Gen. 1–11 the biblical authors were not interpreting facts corresponding to what they wrote but a piece of tradition, an important part of which came from Mesopotamia. With the help of this material they deliver an important message on several levels.

At the oldest level the narratives express a universal and fundamental human experience. Adam, whose name means 'human being', represents all of us: in telling his history we can recognize all of us. In this sense we are all his sons. The same goes for Noah, the sole survivor of the flood and the father of present-day humanity. The same also goes for Cain, or those who built the tower of Babel: throughout, Gen. 1–11 speaks of the whole of humankind and its essential experience, interpreted in a characteristic way.

– Like Adam we are creatures: we began by receiving our being, our life, from God (Gen. 2.7). Everything began with the generosity of the Other who made us. That is quite clear: without our parents we would not be here. But the interpretation of the Bible is that beyond our parents, the life which we have received ultimately comes from God. That invites us to adopt a fundamental attitude of recognition and thanksgiving. Nothing is stranger to the Bible than the modern myth of the self-made man.

– Like Adam or the builders of the tower we experience inherent limits to the human condition. In Gen. 2–3 human beings cannot have access to the tree in the middle of the garden, which represents the place of God; similarly, in Gen. 11 they cannot 'penetrate the heavens' (v.4). Whatever our dreams may be, we shall never be all-powerful, never get beyond our human condition – at least in our own strength. We must accept our human condition, with the great and beautiful things that it contains, but also its limits.

– Like Cain, we all have the experience of a brotherhood broken by violence. We all bear within ourselves aggression against those like us. And this aggression rebounds on us.

– Like Noah, we are all 'saved from the waters'. We have the experi-

ence of an evil which seems to submerge the world: innumerable sufferings, sometimes atrocious deaths, violence of all kinds. But God is
never resigned to evil. On the contrary, the story of the flood shows
that he is the first to combat it, to establish a world which will never
again be ravaged by such a scourge.

– The narratives in Gen. 1–11 thus tell us our history, our experience.
That is their basic meaning. They were then developed along several
lines. The first redactors used them for their political causes: the legitimacy of David (see especially Gen. 9.25, where Canaan is ousted in
favour of his brothers Shem and Japhet, who seem to denote Israel and
the Philistines), then Solomon (see e.g. Gen. 4.1–16*, where YHWH
chooses the younger – like Solomon – in preference to the older – like
Adonijah). From the sixth century on the narrative is included in a
more theological line.

– The Deuteronomistic school reflected on the dramatic experiences
of 598 and 587. Thus it saw the flood as the image of this calamity,
justified by universal wickedness: YHWH strikes only the guilty (6.5),
the sons of Cain whose violence becomes increasingly great (see
4.17–24); as for Noah, he is saved because he is the 'only just man in
his generation' (7.1b). Thus the accent is put on the justice of God,
who brings retribution upon all depending on their condition, but also
on his generosity (thus the gift of clothing to Adam and Eve in 3.21,
or the sign of protection granted to Cain in 4.13–15).

– The Priestly redaction puts the majestic account of creation before
the rest of the text (1.1–2.3). This entrance-hall to the Pentateuch and
the whole Bible shows God in his victorious combat over primitive
chaos; by a series of discreet allusions to the Law, the temple, the
liturgy, or the salvation of Israel it puts the whole of the book under
the sign of a vast hope, that of a world in which everything will be
'good', even 'very good'. On the other hand, P introduces the genealogies of chs. 5 to 11 and emphasizes the divine promises after the
flood (9.1–17*): the whole of history is thus dominated by the blessing and by the faithfulness of God, who will remember his commitment to his people.

– The final redactor of the Pentateuch modifies the text slightly. His
main contributions include the evocation of the four rivers issuing from
paradise (2.10–14), an image of the world made fertile by the Torah.

Genesis 1–11 also takes on different accents from a reading of the New Testament. Thus Christians cannot read the creation narrative without thinking of Jesus Christ, 'the first born of all creation, in whom all things were created' (Col. 1.15–16; cf. John 1.1–18). Similarly, the figure of Adam, the father of all humanity, also expresses its fundamental unity. It attests that we are all brothers. Paul presents Jesus as the new Adam, the father of all humankind (Rom. 5.12–21): he is the human being *par excellence*, the basis of all solidarity; he renews the figure of Adam because he has not shared Adam's sin. The flood prefigures the coming of the Son of Man (see Matt. 24.37–39; Luke 17.26–27). Finally, the story of the tower of Babel finds its conclusion in the outpouring of the Spirit on the day of the first Christian Pentecost (Acts 2.1–13).

The history of the patriarchs (Gen. 12–50)

Abraham, Isaac and Jacob are well-known figures. Or at least we believe they are. In fact we have probably remembered only scraps of their history: the call of Abraham, the sacrifice of Isaac, Jacob's dream at Bethel and the fight by the river Yabbok. But what is the guiding thread of the narrative?

The biblical narrative

Genesis 12–50 does not yet report the history of the Israelite people but that of a family from which Israel will emerge. It is a second pre-amble, after the narrative of origins. We find three blocks in it: the story of Abram-Abraham (11.27–25.18), the story of Israel-Jacob (25.19–37.1) and finally the story of Joseph (37.2–50.26). The story of Isaac is inserted into that of Jacob (ch. 26), and the Jacob story is in fact continued in that of Joseph: the patriarch dies only in chapter 50.

The story of Abraham – who first bears the name Abram – comprises two linked themes: the migration from Mesopotamia to Hebron, marked by a series of promises (11.27–15.21), and the question of the son who will inherit, which begins with the promise (15.1–6), finds a first realization which proves abortive (Ishmael,

ch.16), and finally reaches its culmination with the birth of Isaac
(18.1–15; 21.1–7). Other themes are grafted on to this whole, like that
of Lot, with the destruction of Sodom and Gomorrah (18.16–19.38),
or that of the sacrifice of Isaac (22.1–19).

The story of Israel-Jacob opens with rivalry between the two
brothers (25.19–34; 27.1–45). After robbing Esau of the blessing
which designates the new head of the family, Jacob has to flee: he
arrives at Bethel, where he has his famous dream (28.10–22), and then
he stays with Laban, where he marries and has many children
(29.1–31.21). On the way back he makes a pact with Laban (31.43–
32.2) and then struggles with God while trying to cross the river
Yabbok (32.23–33). Finally the two brothers meet again, but Esau has
lost his aggression; he yields to Jacob, who settles at Shechem
(33.1–20).

The narrative continues with the story of Joseph. Sold by his older
brothers (ch. 37), he arrives in Egypt, where he soon becomes
Pharaoh's trusted adviser and the master of the country (39.1–41.49).
The brothers in turn come to Egypt to buy corn, and prostrate themselves before Joseph, whom they have not recognized (41.50–42.24).
After several journeys by the brothers (Joseph has his younger brother Benjamin brought . . .), the old Jacob also arrives in Egypt
(46.1–47.12). There he dies, after blessing his twelve sons (ch. 49).

> Read Gen. 11.27–15.21; 18.1–15; 22.1–19.
> Read Gen. 25.19–34; 27.1–45; 28.10–22; 32.23–33.
> Read Gen. 37.2–36; 39.1–42.24; 49.1–28.

The facts

It is difficult, if not impossible, to reconstruct the biography of the
patriarchs. In fact it is not easy to distinguish the destiny of the ancestor from that of the group which bears his name. Thus 'Israel' is both
the Israelite people and the patriarch of the same name; to relate the
adventures of this latter is always also, in a way, to talk of the experience of the group which goes back to him. In other words, the patriarchal narratives play a role similar to the narratives in Gen. 1–11:
they are accounts of origins, i.e. myths in the noble sense. When Israel
relates the history of its ancestor (Abraham or Jacob) it identifies with

him and expresses the awareness it has of its relationship to God and other peoples.

That brings us to the question of the genealogy of the patriarchs. In Genesis, Joseph is the son of Jacob, who is himself the son of Isaac and grandson of Abraham. In their primitive oral form, however, the narratives were independent of one another: it was not until the tenth century that they were brought together to form a single literary work. So it is impossible to arrange the four ancestors on a chronological scale. On the other hand, the genealogical tree which includes numerous names of peoples (Kedar, Edom, Midian, Aram, Moab, etc.) allows us to understand how Israel put itself in the political and geographical context of the ancient Near East.

All that has been said so far indicates that it is impossible to locate the patriarchs in a precise period. Abraham's migration is often put at the beginning of the second millennium, around the nineteenth or eighteenth century, but these estimates have no sound basis. The strongest links are those which associate the patriarchs with the Aramaeans, the first clear mention of whom comes from the end of the twelfth century. Even if the Aramaeans were able later to settle in northern Mesopotamia and Transjordan, this date gives some idea of the effective age of the earliest patriarchal traditions: they are almost contemporary with the traditions of the Exodus and the settlement. They come from groups which had not been in Egypt, and the classical sequence (patriarchs, stay in Egypt, Exodus, conquests) results from the juxtaposition of narratives which were initially independent.

The interpretation

The texts are not content to reproduce ancient traditions; they bear witness to a way of understanding them; in turn they are open to multiple interpretations. To illustrate these two realities, let's read the Abraham and Jacob cycles.

The story of Abram-Abraham (Gen. 12–25)

The story of the patriarch is initially orientated on political propaganda in favour of David (promise of the land of Shechem and of Bethel to the descendants of the man of Hebron), and then Solomon (the heritage does not go to Ishmael, but to Isaac, his younger brother). However, the present text is stamped by Elohistic, Deuteronomistic, Priestly and post-Priestly redactions.

The Elohistic story of Abraham extends to chs. 20–22*. It emphasizes above all the moral qualities of the patriarch. He does not lie by presenting his wife as his sister (20.1–18*; compare 26.1–11*); he and Sarah treat Hagar gently (21.8–21; compare 16.1–16* J); he has friendly relations with Abimelech (21.22–34*; compare with 26.26–33*J); finally, subjected to a terrible trial, he remains faithful to the end and thus shows that he 'fears' God (22.1–19*).

The presentation of Abraham as a model of behaviour is again emphasized by the Deuteronomistic redactions from the time of the exile. This time the patriarch shows generosity towards Lot, to whom he leaves the best territory (13.7–11a); with a small force he defeats the four great kings and delivers Lot, but refuses to enrich himself (14.1–24*); he puts his trust in YHWH, who promises him an innumerable posterity (15.5–6); he intercedes boldly on behalf of Sodom (18.22–32). This faithfulness is recompensed by YHWH, who gives him his blessing (12.2–3*), i.e. fertility: he will be the father of an innumerable posterity (15.5; 22.5–18).

The P contribution emphasizes another aspect of Abraham's behaviour: circumcision (17.1–26*). The patriarch is admirable not only for his moral conduct but also because he is a faithful 'observer'.

The final redactor completes the picture by adding two new qualities: Abraham pays a tithe to the priest of God Most High, the king of Salem, who represents the high priest (14.18–20), and ensures that his son does not marry a wife 'from among the daughters of the Canaanites', but a woman from his own family who has remained in Mesopotamia (a rejection of 'mixed marriages', ch. 24).

In the New Testament, Abraham is above all the 'father of the faithful', a man of exemplary faith (Rom. 4; Gal. 3.6–29; James 2.21–23; Heb. 11.8–10). Paul refers several times to Gen. 15.6: 'Abraham believed in YHWH and it was reckoned to him as righteousness'. We can re-read the whole of Gen. 12–25 considering the various dimensions of Abraham's faith:

– This faith is a journey, an exodus. The narrative opens (Gen. 12.1) with the order to depart. Abraham knows what he is leaving but not what he will find. He has to leave 'his country, his kinsfolk and his father's house', i.e. his own roots. Faith begins by his tearing himself away to embark on an adventure which is out of his control. Joshua 24.2–3 spells this out: Abraham leaves idolatry to receive true faith. This departure is the first in a long series. When he is finally at home with a child who replaces his family lost in Mesopotamia, he is called on to sacrifice his son (ch. 22). So Abraham goes through deprivation after deprivation. Will he never know rest? The only fixed place that he owns is the field of Machpelah, which will serve him as a tomb (ch. 23). He will have been journeying, seeking, until his dying day. When he dies, the narrator states that he was 'gathered to his people' (25.8); this suggests that the successive departures, far from crippling him, have restored him to himself. Faith is a way but not an evasion; it leads us to discover ourselves at great depth. Along the same lines, the New Testament presents the believer as the one who follows Jesus on the way he risked, who undertakes to go with him to Jerusalem, the place of the passion and the resurrection.

– Faith is a welcoming of the divine grace. Gal. 3 and Rom. 4 emphasize that the faith of Abraham precedes his observance of the Law; it consists in accepting the gift of God revealed by his promises. These promises are expressed in Gen. 12–23, with three dimensions: the gift of fertility, divine protection and a bringing together in unity of 'all the families of the heart'. Abraham will bear a blessing for the whole of humanity. Later we find a last object of the promise: the gift of the land. In the New Testament both the Synoptic Gospels and John or the Pauline literature equally emphasize the primacy of grace over merits. Jesus begins the fulfilment of the promise: wherever he goes, the kingdom of God takes form and is given unconditionally to all. At the same time Jesus deepens the promise, for the kingdom is as yet given only as a prefiguration, an example. The believer is the one who accepts this kingdom as good news.

– Faith is also obedience and thus openness to the Law. The biblical narrative emphatically presents Abraham as a model of faithfulness to the divine will. That does not prevent him from having a particularly bold dialogue with YHWH before the destruction of Sodom (18.22–33).

The Jacob cycle

It is possible to reconstruct a literary and theology history of the Jacob cycle parallel to that of the Abraham cycle. Other approaches to the text are also legitimate. Here I suggest a more anthropological type of reading.

Genesis 25–36 relates above all the story of twin brothers, who oppose each other violently and finally are reconciled. A long separation and a confrontation between Jacob and Laban and Jacob and his God (the Yabbok episode, 32.23–33) are necessary to arrive at this denouement.

In Gen. 4 the reader has already encountered a story of rival brothers: the narrative of the murder of Abel by Cain. The confrontation between Esau and Jacob has more than one point in common with this story. Are we going to see, like the first time, the murder of the younger brother by the older? No, the conflict will end with the reconciliation of the rivals and their peaceful co-existence. In other words, the narrative relates how brotherhood is possible, beyond frustrations and confrontations.

At the starting point the situation is even more serious than in chapter 4. Cain was a peaceful farmer and Abel a peaceful shepherd, and their conflict arose out of a decision from outside: the choice of YHWH, who preferred the latter to the former. Nevertheless, Cain's frustration leads to murder. Here the two brothers are at war from their mother's womb (25.22–23). We foresee the worst, all the more so since the two figures are both notable for their greed. Esau is a hunter: he tracks animals down and does not hesitate to shed their blood; on his first appearance he is presented as famished, ready to do anything for a bite to eat (25.29–34). Jacob is his twin brother, his double. Though he is a shepherd, he literally puts himself under the hunter's skin to steal his privileges from him (ch. 27). Like Cain, Esau is dispossessed of the fertile land. Worse, he is going to have to serve his brother, and he will live by his sword (27.39–40). So he will be the man of violence, and it is not surprising that he watches out to kill Jacob (v.41). However, the murder will not take place: at the end of the narrative the two brothers are reconciled. But to get that far each has had to travel a long road.

The twins must first of all be separated. That is the advice that Rebecca gives Jacob (27.43–45). This separation lasts for years, and when the two brothers finally meet again, their ways immediately diverge (33.16–20). That is the condition of their co-existence: they must not be too close to each other. As twins living in the same space they can only be rivals. No brotherhood is possible unless a good distance has been established: too far from each other, the brothers would end by being strangers to each other; too close and they would risk killing each other.

Then they have to speak. During the scene with the mess of pottage (25.29–34) the brothers had held a basic conversation, but sufficient for the desires of each to co-exist: each had been able to get what he sought. In the episode in ch. 27 the brothers do not exchange a single word: once the theft has been perpetrated, anger prevents any dialogue. Dialogue is only resumed years later, first of all by ambassadors sent on in advance (32.4–7) and then face to face (33.5–16). Only then is reconciliation possible. In the end, violence always marks failure or the absence of words.

For fratricidal hatred to give place to peace, Jacob too has to pursue an inner way. He flees because he fears his brother's violence. To get over his fear he has to have other encounters, beginning with that with his God. The encounter takes place three times: at Bethel on the route of his flight (28.10–22), then at the house of Laban (31.3, 11–31), and finally at Penuel, on the return journey (32.23–33).

– At Bethel Jacob receives a fundamental assurance from God: 'I shall be with you, I shall preserve you wherever you go, and I will bring you back to this land' (28.15). So Jacob knows that he is not left to himself; Yahweh will continue to show his favour, and promises that he will return to the land where Esau still is: doesn't that indicate that a reconciliation is possible and that it will indeed take place?
– At the house of Laban (ch. 29–30) the deceiver is deceived in his turn! He experiences the feelings of his own victim. The conflict between Jacob and Laban can be resolved only by a bitter conversation in which each dares to tell the other how he feels (31.26–42). Once the storm is past, reconciliation is possible by dividing up each person's territory. We can imagine that this experience allowed the

patriarch to envisage his impending meeting with Esau in a positive light.

– On the return journey, when the confrontation with Esau is imminent, Jacob struggles all night with the mysterious being of the river (32.23–33). The patriarch replays the theft of the paternal blessing – with significant modifications. In Gen. 27 he put himself under Esau's skin; now he says his own name. He dares to be himself without hiding behind another. Then he is given a new name: he is no longer 'the supplanter' (*ya'aqob*) but a new man, freed from his guilt. Thus transformed, Jacob–Israel can receive as a gift (v.30b) the blessing which he stole from his brother, snatched from his father by a trick. From now on he is no longer afraid: he goes to the head of his group and presents himself directly to Esau (33.1–3).

Even if the text does not say anything about it, Esau, too, seems to have had to make a journey, from his desire to kill his brother (27.41) to the renunciation of an intention to do him harm. Whereas Cain did not succeed in killing the savage beast within him, Esau did.

The story of Esau and Jacob adds two things to that of Cain and Abel. First, it shows that it is too simple to divide society into executioners and victims. Here the complexity of human feelings is evident: in the end Esau, the hunter, is less aggressive than Jacob, the shepherd. Secondly, this narrative makes it possible to give the history of fratricidal violence a happy ending. It is not said that rivalry between brothers always ends up in murder! Reconciliation is possible, but it requires certain conditions.

The history of Moses (Exodus-Deuteronomy)

The heart of the foundation myth of Israel is the story of the exodus from Egypt and the gift of the promised land, as this is summed up in Deut. 6.21–23: 'We were Pharaoh's slaves in Egypt and YHWH brought us out of Egypt with a mighty hand; and YHWH showed signs and wonders, great and grievous, against Egypt and against Pharaoh and all his household, before our eyes; and he brought us out from there, that he might bring us in and give us the land which he swore to give to our fathers.' We can distinguish two essential aspects of the myth: the departure from the land of slavery under the leadership of Moses, and the entry into the land of prosperity under the leadership of Joshua. The former will be considered here, the latter in the next section.

The biblical narrative

The story of Moses takes up a great deal of room, comprising the books of Exodus, Leviticus, Numbers and Deuteronomy. The narrative framework of this complex has been enriched by other material which amounts to a considerable body: above all the laws (Ex. 20–23, but also the greater part of Leviticus, several chapters of Numbers and Deut. 12–26) and long speeches by Moses (which form the greater part of Deuteronomy). The following elements can be distinguished in the narrative: the departure from Egypt and the beginning of the journey through the wilderness (Ex. 1–18); the stay on Sinai with the concluding of the covenant and the gift of the Law (Ex. 19–Num. 10); and finally the journey through the wilderness to the threshold of the promised land (Num. 11-Deut. 34).

In the first part of the narrative (Ex. 1–18), the narrator describes the increasingly dramatic situation of the people, who are suffering real persecution from Pharaoh. Moses has to flee far from his people. In his exile, he receives from YHWH the mission to free them (the scene at the burning bush). With Aaron his brother he several times goes to see Pharaoh to convince him to let Israel go, but comes up against a series of refusals. Each refusal is punished by a misfortune (the 'plagues of Egypt'). Finally the Destroyer strikes all the firstborn of the Egyptians, whereas the Israelites are protected by the Passover rite. After this decisive blow, Pharaoh lets Israel go. Soon, however, he regrets his decision and sets out with his chariots in pursuit of the people, whose route is barred by the sea. Once again YHWH intervenes: he brings Israel to the shore of freedom, while the Egyptian army is swallowed up in the waters. The journey through the wilderness can then take place, punctuated by the murmuring of the people.

Read Ex. 1–4; 12.21–42; 13.17–15.21.

On arrival at Sinai, Israel witnesses a great theophany: YHWH manifests himself in a storm and a volcanic eruption (Ex. 19); he reveals his Law, beginning with the Decalogue (20.2–17), which is supplemented by other regulations (20.24–23.33). The people promises to be faithful to it and commits itself to the covenant (24.3–8). Moses then climbs the mountain; he receives the instructions for the wilderness sanctuary and the tables written with God's own finger (chs. 25–31). Meanwhile Israel is worshipping the golden calf (32.1–14), thus breaking the covenant to which it had committed itself on the very first day. The tables are broken, but YHWH allows Moses to receive new ones (32.15–34.35). The end of the book of Exodus relates the building of the wilderness sanctuary (chs. 35–40). Leviticus then expounds a series of rules relating to the ritual of sacrifices (chs. 1–7), the investiture of priests (chs. 8–10), what is clean and what is unclean (chs. 11–16: regulations about food, leprosy, etc.) and finally the 'Holiness Code', by which the people is to distinguish itself from other nations (chs. 17–26, with an appendix on the rules for fulfilling vows, ch. 27). The book of Numbers opens with an account of the great census (chs. 1–4) and expounds several laws (chs.5–8). Finally, after the celebration of the Passover, the people sets out again (chs. 9–10).

Read Ex. 19.1–20,21; 24.1–18; 32–34; Lev. 11; 19.

From Num. 11 onwards, the people has resumed its journey in the direction of the Promised Land. As during the first part of the way, this journey is marked by various trials. Thus the spies sent out to reconnoitre the land return saying that it is inhabited by giants (Num. 13). The people rebel, and YHWH punishes them: they are condemned to forty years of wandering in the wilderness (ch. 14). Another important episode is the encounter with Balaam, a pagan magician sent by the king of Moab to curse Israel: instead of cursing them, he blesses them (chs. 22–24). This second part of the book of Numbers contains more legislative sections, relating above all to the liturgy (chs. 15–19; 26–30; 35–36).

Read Num. 13–14; 22–24.

Deuteronomy presents itself as being almost entirely the farewell speech of Moses. Israel is going to cross the Jordan, but Moses will die on Mount Nebo; he will see the Promised Land only from the distance. The old man recalls all that has happened since Egypt and calls on the people to observe the Law: that is the condition for the people to be able to live long in its land. In the middle of this speech there is a collection of laws known as the 'Deuteronomic Code' (chs. 12–26). Moses expounds the blessings and curses attached to the observance or non-observance of this law (chs. 27–28). He ends his speech by confronting Israel with a choice on which its very life depends (ch. 30). The book ends with several gestures on the part of Moses: he hands on his authority to Joshua, sings a song bearing witness to the commitment of the people, and blesses the twelve tribes (chs. 31–33). Finally readers witness the death of the hero (ch. 34).

Read Deut. 4–6; 12–13; 28.1–46; 30.15–20.

The facts

For the best present-day historians, the stay in the region of Egypt only involved a small number of people, and certainly not the twelve tribes. Semitic populations, of the class of *'Apiru* or 'Hebrews', led a semi-nomadic life in the steppes east of the Nile Delta.

Almost certainly it was Ramses II (1290–1224) who towards the end of his reign sought to exercise better control over these turbulent populations by using them for his great works. Exodus 1.8 speaks of the building of Pithom and above all Pi-Ramses, this Pharaoh's ephemeral capital. The conscript 'Hebrews' sought to escape this form of slavery and fled. Moses must have been the leader of this movement. The fugitives spent some time in the wilderness, where they experienced many trials (skirmishes with elements of the Egyptian army, hunger and thirst, etc.). But we need not imagine a great people on the march with a precise itinerary. Among the places remembered in the ancient tradition is Mount Sinai, which is generally situated at the south of the peninsula of the same name.

The 'Apiru

Texts from various regions of the Near East and from all periods between the end of the third millennium and around the year 1000 speak of a population called *'Apiru* or Hapiru. These people are of Semitic origin. They are always regarded as foreigners, with an inferior status. They are semi-nomads living on the edge of the desert, or mercenaries. At any event, they live on the periphery of 'civilized' society and have only limited rights. For a long time now the word *'Apiru* has been connected with the Hebrew word *'ibri*. This term appears thirty-three times in the Hebrew Bible, where it denotes the people of Israel; it is usually translated 'Hebrew'. However, it should be noted that this usage is limited and that the term is often put in the mouth of foreigners or Israelites addressing foreigners. Apart from a few late texts, the term 'Hebrew' does not denote Israel as an ethnic group but rather membership of the social class of the *'Apiru*.

The interpretation

The event of the Exodus need not have been particularly spectacular. However, for those who experienced it and for later Israelite memory this was *the* event, the starting point of a vast adventure.

At the very moment when all this was happening, the Israelites interpreted it as liberation from slavery, attributing it to YHWH, the God attached to their group. This was the birth of the Israelite confession of faith: YHWH our God is our liberator! He is not tied to the powerful of this world but has made us, who were slaves, a people of free men and women. This experience of encounter with a God who raises up those who have been humiliated and hears the cries of those who can do no more (cf. Ex. 3.7–8) marked the Israelite consciousness for ever. It was to be extended in the witness and action of Jesus, who opens the kingdom of God to the little ones, the sick, public sinners and the marginalized of all kinds.

Freedom from slavery is celebrated in the liturgy: the ritual actually features in the narrative of the book of Exodus: 'Select lambs for yourselves according to your families, and kill the Passover lamb. Take a bunch of hyssop and dip it in the blood which is in the basin, and touch the lintel and the two doorposts with the blood which is in the basin . . .' (Ex. 12.21–22). These gestures represent an ancient rite of semi-nomads who each spring would sacrifice a lamb to ensure the prosperity of the flock and smeared the tops of their tents with its blood to avert evil powers, 'the Destroyer'. In the Israelite liturgy they no longer have the same significance; from now on they celebrate YHWH, the God who frees the oppressed. The same goes for the other religious festivals. The Feast of Unleavened Bread, associated with Passover because it was celebrated at the same time of year, similarly celebrates the departure form Egypt; Pentecost, celebrated fifty days later, commemorates the covenant; the Feast of Booths or Tabernacles in the autumn revives life in tents in the wilderness (for the liturgical calendar see pp. 134f. below). The biblical narrative relates the wonders of God, which are sung and 'lived out' in the liturgy.

The account of the liberation ends up with the gift of the Law at the theophany on Sinai. In the biblical perspective, observing the Law does not mean being imprisoned in regulations which limit freedom: on the contrary, the Law is the charter of a free people, its plan for living. Thus the Decalogue which forms the heart of the Law does not begin with a commandment but with a word of revelation: 'I am YHWH your God who brought you up from the land of Egypt, from the house of slavery' (Ex. 20.2; Deut. 5.6). God gives his Law to Israel so that its freedom shall be effective, not only on a political level but also on the level of the moral conscience. By virtue of its content, it brings freedom from the inner slavery of idolatry and protects the weak, rejecting any new form of servitude. That is the character of the two tables of the Law, the hinge of which is the commandment about the sabbath. On the one hand the observance of the sabbath is linked to the memory of the creation in six days, with the seventh day reserved for YHWH's rest (Ex. 20.11). On the other its aim is to allow the worker to rest, so that his work does not overwhelm him (Deut. 5.14; cf. Ex. 23.12). It is given this commentary: 'You shall remember that you were a slave in the land of Egypt and the Lord your God brought you thence with a mighty hand and outstretched arm' (Deut. 5.15). Certainly the Law contains various rules about slaves: thus such legislation accepts slavery as a fact. However, it also sets limits to it (Ex. 21.1–11, 20–21, 26–27; Lev. 25.35–55; Deut. 15.12–18).

Originally the Decalogue and the other collections of laws were independent of any narrative framework; this was simply the law in force. In the current biblical narrative the Law is given by YHWH to Israel at the time of the theophany on Sinai, in the framework of the concluding of a covenant. This presentation of the facts is the work of the Deuteronomistic school, which thus offers a key to the interpretation of the whole of later history. In his generosity YHWH has not only given Israel material freedom but has also offered it privileged relations of trust in the framework of a pact: he himself has assured Israel security and happiness on condition that Israel is faithful to his Law. Israel entered into this agreement freely (Ex. 19.3b-8; 24.3–8), but immediately betrayed it (the worship of the golden calf, Ex. 32). YHWH forgives his guilty people: he reveals himself as a 'God merciful and gracious, slow to anger, and abounding in steadfast love and faithfulness' (Ex. 34.6). Israel shows no recognition of YHWH. On the contrary, it will constantly betray him, so that eventually YHWH resolves to strike it: in the eyes of the Deuteronomists that explains the terrible misfortunes of their time. The covenant is not a specific historical event, but rather an interpretative category by which the Deuteronomistic school expresses its faith in a just and good God despite the accusations made against him.

So the covenant is broken by Israel's lack of trust and idolatry. According to the terms of the agreement, this misconduct must be punished by death, as is indicated by the gesture of the sprinkling of blood in Ex. 24.8. So YHWH punishes the guilty people, but he himself sets a term for their misfortune, signified by their time in the wilderness: this will last forty years, so that the guilty generation is eliminated, but the innocent generation regains happiness (cf. Deut. 1.35–39). Moses' great farewell speech, which comprises almost the whole of Deuteronomy (1.6–30.20), bears witness to this: the covenant of Horeb has been broken, but YHWH tells Israel that he will renew it (covenant of Moab, Deut. 28.9–20). As at the first time, the divine offer has arisen out of great need, and Moses reiterates calls for faithfulness, in particular to worship only YHWH. Behind this presentation we can recognize faith in a God who is always generous, who constantly wants to hope in his people despite their failings.

Within this framework, new literary elements are introduced by the Priestly school (P). From now on Moses is associated with Aaron, the 'father' of all priests, and he himself becomes a priestly figure. The laws are supplemented by long descriptions of the wilderness sanctuary and the liturgy. All this is further reinforced by the final redactor of the Pentateuch. The theophany on Sinai is understood as a vast liturgical celebration in which a distinction is made between the people, who remain at the bottom of the mountain; the ordinary priests, who climb it; and finally Moses, the high-priestly figure, who goes right to the top and meets YHWH face to face (cf. Ex. 19.20–23). Along the same lines, the Law is dominated by the book of Leviticus, with its emphasis on the distinction between clean and unclean (food laws, laws on leprosy, etc.), sacred and profane.

The traditional Christian interpretation sees the work of Moses as the outline of that of Christ. Is he not the liberator *par excellence*, who snatches humanity, and Israel in particular, from its own slavery? He reveals the new Law, which is not a substitute for the Mosaic Law but brings it to fulfilment (Matt. 5.17). From now on the passage through the sea (Ex. 14–15) symbolizes the resurrection: it is a new creation, the transition from death to life; by baptism, which reproduces this passage through the waters of death, the one who has encountered Christ rises with him and attains to true freedom.

Throughout history, oppressed groups have read the exodus as a promise of their liberation. Thus the black American slaves spoke of freedom as a Promised Land beyond the Jordan. Similarly, encouraged by the liberation theologians, the Latin American base communities identify with the people of Israel in subjection in Egypt, but soon liberated by God and travelling to the land of happiness.

The history of Joshua

As Deuteronomy announces, Joshua is to complete the work of Moses by crossing the Jordan with Israel and taking possession of the Promised Land. Freedom from slavery in Egypt is matched by entry into another land, that of happiness and freedom.

The biblical narrative

The book of Joshua presents the penetration of Canaanite territory as an easy and rapid conquest, made by all Israel under the orders of Joshua. After going round the Dead Sea and crossing the Jordan (chs. 1–5), the Israelites annihilate the forces opposing their triumphal advance. They capture Jericho (ch. 6) and then Ai (chs. 7–8), but make a treaty with Gibeon: terrified by Israel, the Gibeonites submit voluntarily (ch. 9). The Israelites are thus masters of the whole of central Palestine. Then they conquer a coalition of the five kings of the South (ch. 10) and a coalition of the kings of the North (ch. 11). Chapter 12 forms the conclusion of the first part of the book with a list of the thirty-one conquered kings.

A second section outlines the division of the territory between the twelve tribes (chs. 13–21) and then the return of two and a half tribes to Transjordan (ch. 22). The work ends with a speech by Joshua (ch. 23) and then an assembly in Shechem, where the people commit themselves to YHWH in the covenant (24.1–28). Last comes the narrative of the death of Joshua (24.1–33).

Read Josh. 6; 10; 24.

The facts

The account of the facts in the book of Joshua is certainly stylized and stamped by the theology of the redactors. The biblical narrative itself shows the historical improbability of the conquest of all the land by 'all Israel' led by Joshua. In fact Judg. 1.10, 21, 27–35 gives a very different account of the same events: it is not 'all Israel' but each tribe separately which takes possession of its own territory; the figure of Joshua is passed over in silence; finally, entire regions escape Israelite control. It is certain that such a note is closer to the facts than the grandiose picture in the book of Joshua.

That having been said, what actually happened on the ground? The emergence of Israel has been the object of several theories (military conquest, peaceful infiltration, brutal revolution, social evolution without notable violence), all of which can take advantage of some

features in the biblical text. Moreover, it may be that each one has part
of the truth, since the settlement of Israel took different forms in
different regions. At all events, archaeology shows the creation of
numerous new localities both in the hill-country of central Palestine
and in the hill-country of Judah from the twelfth century on, and it is
on an Egyptian stele dated 1207 that we first encounter the name
'Israel'. A new civilization came to birth in a context disturbed by the
upheavals which affected the whole region: its twofold origin lay in
the old local Canaanite population and groups which had come from
Egypt, bearing faith in YHWH as a liberating God. In a second phase
(the eleventh century), the tribes of Galilee in turn freed themselves
from the Canaanite petty kings and also adopted faith in YHWH;
perhaps the same battle is described in Josh. 1.1–14 (Joshua's victory
with 'all Israel' over Jabin king of Hazor at the 'waters of Merom') and
Judg. 4–5 (the victory of Barak over Sisera, Jabin's general, on Mount
Tabor and by the 'waters of Megiddo'). For an overall view see the
account on pp. 33f. above.

The interpretation

The Joshua narrative is stamped by three dominant traits: it presents
events as if they concerned 'all Israel'; it describes the 'war of YHWH',
and finally it is impregnated with ritualism. The first two features
come from the Deuteronomistic school and the third from the final
redactor of the Pentateuch in the Persian period.

First of all, the book of Joshua is stamped by pan-Israelism: it is the
whole people, composed of the twelve tribes, which advances in a
single group under the authority of Moses' successor. The aim of this
presentation, which does not correspond to the facts, is to provide a
common origin for the different elements of Israel: 'all' were in Egypt,
'all' were freed by YHWH, 'all' received their land from him, 'all'
committed themselves to serving only YHWH. Over against this unified
people we find the multiplicity of local populations, 'Hittites, Amorites,
Canaanites, Perizzites, Hivites and Jebusites' (9.1), led by a large
number of kings (see the list in ch. 12). The experience of the exodus
makes Israel a unique people, which cannot mix with other peoples.

The work of liberation by which YHWH had delivered Israel from slavery in Egypt continued in the Promised Land. Just as YHWH had conquered Pharaoh with the miracle by the sea (Ex. 14–15), so he gave Israel victory over the pagan kings of Canaan. The land was not conquered; it was given by YHWH, as is forcibly emphasized by Josh. 24.13. Jericho, the impregnable city, falls simply as the result of a ritual procession (ch. 6); similarly, the victory of Gibeon is made possible because the sun stands still (10.10–13). The divine action only requires Israel to trust in its God. Every victory is punctuated by the ban; the local population is put to the sword (6.17–21; 8.26–29; 10.28–39; 11.10–23); when the ban is not respected, the divine anger falls on Israel (7.1–26). Behind this presentation of events we must read a concern not to be contaminated in any way by paganism. That corresponds to the concern of the Deuteronomistic school, which regarded idolatry as the major cause of the misfortunes of 598 and 587; to prosper it is necessary to remain faithful to the one God and therefore not to have any contact with the pagan world. That is the demand of the covenant.

Finally, the account as we have it is stamped by the liturgy. The people who are taking possession of 'their' land are not drawn up like a military force but advance in procession: they are preceded by the priests bearing the ark when they cross the Jordan (chs. 3–4). In fact the river forms the boundary of a 'holy land', a vast sanctuary (see 5.15), and Israel plays the role of the priest, who has access to this sacred zone. Similarly, it is after a solemn procession that the walls of Jericho fall down. The sharing out of the land between the tribes (chs. 13–20) does not follow from the military exploits of each group, since all Israel fought together: it follows from drawing of lots 'in the presence of YHWH, at the opening of the Tent of Meeting' (20.51). Thus Israel is not a people like others, but a liturgical community whose roles are fixed by YHWH.

The Christian reading of the book of Joshua sees it as a continuation of the book of Exodus. Moses' successor brings Israel into the Promised Land and invites it to engage in the covenant. These two features already announce the work of Jesus, who opens up the kingdom and brings the people into it in the new covenant.

The history of the judges

Between the time of the 'conquest' and that of the monarchy the Bible puts the time of the judges (*šopᵉtim*, better translated 'leaders', since the *šopēt* is the one who takes a decision).

The biblical narrative

The book of Judges reports the actions of a series of characters who have to be divided into two groups. Six of them are given only a brief mention; that is why they are called the 'minor judges' (Shamgar, Tola, Jair, Ibzan, Elon and Abdon, Judg. 3.31; 10.1–5; 12.8–15). Six others are the object of a developed narrative: Othniel, Ehud, Barak, and above all Gideon (6.1–9.57), Jephthah (10.6–12.7) and Samson (13.1–16.31). These are military leaders, the 'liberators' who deliver Israel from an external danger and then govern it until their death. This period is presented as a succession of cycles comprising the same stages: the unfaithfulness of Israel, the anger of YHWH and the distress of Israel, divine compassion, the sending of judges who deliver Israel; and then, after the death of the judge, new unfaithfulness on the part of Israel (Judg. 2.11–19).

The story of the judges is continued in the first book of Samuel, in which Samuel himself plays a major role. His exceptional destiny is evident from his miraculous birth, since his mother Hannah was barren. Samuel was called by God when he was attached to the temple in Shiloh (chs. 1–3). Later he liberates Israel from the yoke of the Philistines and becomes a judge (ch. 8). At the end of his life he anoints Saul (I Sam. 9–10) and David (I Sam. 16.1–13) king. Samuel is also presented as a prophet.

> Read Judg. 2.11–3.6; 4–5; 7; I Sam. 1–3; 7.

The facts

The account in the book of Judges corresponds to the stage of consolidation which saw the emergence of Israel, as this was described in an earlier chapter. Several of the 'minor judges' bear the names of clans: each time the notes indicate where the judge is buried. The historical existence of these characters is improbable; the listing of them is almost certainly to be seen as a list of the tombs of sheikhs of the kind that can be found almost all over the Near East.

The narratives about the 'major judges' are of a different kind. This time the texts take up old traditions, and some elements in the text derive from historical reminiscences. However, contrary to the presentation of the book, the action of the *šopᵉtim* was local, with the participation of limited groups. These were the wartime leaders, who from time to time intervened in the face of a particular danger. The twelfth century was in fact a period when the Israelite tribes were fighting on several fronts: they were facing the last Canaanite city states, defending their territory from foreign groups (Philistines in the west and Ammonites and Moabites in the east) and fighting among themselves (cf. Judg. 19–21, the war between Ephraim and Benjamin).

To begin with, the Israelite tribes were independent of one another. Gradually they came to form two groups, around Ephraim in the north and Judah in the south. This development, which ended soon after the year 1000 with the establishment of the monarchy, was fed by the feeling of having the same ethnic background, by sharing a common faith in YHWH and by the imperatives of collective security; to this we must add the ambition of certain individuals.

Historically, Samuel was certainly a seer (cf. I Sam. 9.6–21) who played some role at the court of Saul (see I Sam. 10.20–27); the historicity of his military exploits remains doubtful.

The interpretation

Like the book of Joshua, the book of Judges is stamped with the theology of the Deuteronomistic school. It is not surprising to find the same pan-Israelite perspective and the same representations of the 'war of YHWH' (see e.g. Judg. 7). The narrative employs a characteristic theology of history: when left to itself the people always sinks into idolatry, thus breaking the covenant with YHWH. This explains all the foreign invasions. Happily YHWH does not abandon his people to their distress: he sends them saviours who give them freedom and educate them in faithfulness. In a way, each judge is a new Moses.

YHWH reveals himself as a faithful and patient God who punishes his people whenever they sin, in conformity with the covenant, but who each time rescues them in sheer compassion.

It should be added that, for the Deuteronomists, the judges embody the ideal of good government, as opposed to the kings, who failed. The kings are represented by Jerubbaal-Abimelech, the Canaanite sovereign of Shechem (ch. 9), who comes to power after assassinating seventy members of his family. Jotham tells a parable about him in which the monarchy appears as the exercise of destructive power (vv.7–15); Abimelech also massacres all the inhabitants of Shechem (vv.42–49). The judge Gideon, Abimelech's father, had behaved quite differently: he refused royal power, 'for YHWH must reign' over Israel (8.23); Gideon himself, however, had involved his people in an idolatrous cult (8.24–27). Similarly, I Sam. 8 and 12 emphasize the contrast between the judge Samuel, who is a ruler after YHWH's heart, and the king for which Israel calls. This critical view of the institution of the monarchy is quite understandable after the ruin of the Davidic dynasty.

6

The period of the monarchy

The period of the monarchy, which extends from around 1020 to 587 BCE, is the golden age of ancient Israel. The reigns of Saul (the first Israelite king), David (the founder of the great Jerusalem dynasty) and Solomon (the builder of the temple) are still in a way part of the foundation period of Israel. They will be our main concern. The account of the other reigns will be briefer; finally we must consider a very important phenomenon, 'classical' prophecy.

The history of Saul and David

The story of the first king of Israel and the first king of Judah is told in two long narratives (from I Sam. 8 to I Kings 2; I Chron. 9–29). The length of these texts bears witness to the importance of these figures in the memory of Israel.

The biblical narrative

In the books of Samuel, the advent of the first king of Israel is the subject of four successive narratives: the people call for a king despite the divine warnings (I Sam. 8); Saul secretly receives royal unction at the hands of Samuel (9.1–10.16); designated by the drawing of lots, he is acclaimed king by the crowd (10.17–27); he is proclaimed king by the people after delivering Jabesh-gilead (ch. 11). Saul very quickly loses the initiative: he comes into conflict with his son Jonathan and the people support the latter (chs. 13–14); then he is rejected by

YHWH for not having observed the ban during the war against the Amalekites (ch. 15); Samuel then goes to anoint a new king secretly, namely David son of Jesse (16.1–13), who enters Saul's service as a minstrel and shield-bearer (16.14–23). David defeats the giant Philistine Goliath (ch. 7). Following this exploit, he is promoted to general and marries Saul's daughter (ch. 18). All this gives him great popularity, which irritates Saul. The king wants to eliminate David: when he does not succeed in assassinating him (chs. 20–21), he pursues him across the wilderness with his army (chs. 22–26). Finally, David, who has assembled a personal troop, takes refuge in Gath, among the Philistines, and puts himself at their service (ch. 27). When the Philistines attack Israel, however, he leaves to make war on the Amalekites in the south (chs. 29–30). Saul for his part is disturbed: he consults the ghost of Samuel, who announces his death (ch. 28). His army is in fact beaten on Mount Gilboa and he and his son Jonathan die in battle (I Sam. 31; II Sam. 1).

On the death of Saul, David becomes king of Judah at Hebron, while Abner, the dead king's general, confers the crown on Ishbaal, son of Saul, at Mahanaim in Transjordan (II Sam. 2.1–11). War breaks out between the two states and David gets the upper hand (2.12–3.1). After the murder of Abner and Ishbaal (3.6–4.12), the elders of Israel go to Hebron to make David their ruler (5.1–3). From now on David is king of Judah and Israel. He captures the fortress of Zion (Jerusalem) and installs himself in it (5.1–12); then he has the ark brought up there (ch. 6). Meanwhile he wins a decisive victory over the Philistines (5.17–25) and will also subject other peoples (ch. 8). These successes are interrupted by the oracle of the prophet Nathan, in which YHWH promises him an eternal house (dynasty) (ch. 7).

David is less glorious in the rest of the narrative. During the siege of Rabbah, capital of the Ammonites, the king becomes enamoured of the beautiful Bathsheba; he makes an arrangement with general Joab that her husband, Uriah, shall fall in battle; Solomon is born of the union of David and Bathsheba (II Sam. 10–12). Chapters 13–19 relate the story of Absalom, another son of David, the murderer of his half-brother Amnon. From now on he is heir to the crown. Power will come to him, but he cannot wait; with a band of malcontents he seizes

Jerusalem and David has to flee; Absalom is eventually killed and the king regains his power. Another revolt, that of Sheba, is nipped in the bud (ch. 20). Finally David dies, after placing Solomon on the throne.

> Read I Sam. 8–11; 16–18; 24; II Sam. 7; 11–12; 15.6–19.9.

The facts

What do the historians say about Saul and David? The essentials have already been related earlier (pp. 36 f.). Doubtless both these characters were violent and unscrupulous men. Above all they remained soldiers. Although we cannot be certain, their reigns probably overlapped for some time, one ruling in central Palestine and the other in the south. Were the assassinations of Abner and Ishbaal ordered by David himself? Be this as it may, it was the disappearance of the leaders of Israel which allowed David to exercise his authority over the tribes of the old kingdom of Saul; these tribes must have regarded the man from Hebron as a foreign tyrant. On the other hand, the extent of what some historians call 'David's empire' has doubtless been exaggerated.

The interpretation

At the origins of the vast fresco which runs from I Sam. 8 to I Kings 2 there certainly lie two accounts which were composed during the lifetime of David. The first shows that the way in which the king took power over the old kingdom of Saul was quite legitimate (from I Sam. 11 to II Sam. 7); the second is a history of Absalom (II Sam. 13–20*). The two narratives were brought together and completed under Solomon (from I Sam. 9 to I Kings 2*). These writings, with some narratives from Genesis and Exodus, constitute the earliest literary works in the Bible. Their aim is above all political: they seek to show that the power claimed by David comes from YHWH and cannot be challenged. In this framework the portrait of the king is already beginning to be idealized.

The present narrative of the books of Samuel contrasts the first two sovereigns as far as it can. After his initial exploits Saul immediately misbehaves: he offers the holocaust reserved for the priests (I Sam. 13), he does not observe the law of the ban (I Sam. 15), he wants to kill David, who is innocent (I Sam. 18.10–11.25; 19.1–17, etc.); he massacres the priests of Nob (I Sam. 22); and finally he practises necromancy (I Sam. 28). Saul has a great many grave faults, and that explains his failure. In this presentation we can recognize the Deuteronomistic theology of retribution: it is utterly just that YHWH removes the first king of Israel.

By contrast David has all the qualities. The redactors, who were contemporaries of the king, already sought to present their hero in the most favourable light. For them, the success of David relates less to his attitude than to the favour of YHWH, who accompanies him all along his way (I Sam. 16.18; 17.37; 18.14, 28). The various agents in the narrative recognize that he has a right to the monarchy (Saul, I Sam. 18.8; Ahimelech, I Sam. 22.14; Jonathan, I Sam. 23.17; Abner, II Sam. 3.9–10; Nathan, II Sam. 7.11bβ, 16). He exercises power over the old kingdom of Saul quite legally: predestined from his youth (I Sam. 16.18), he benefits from the abdication of Jonathan, who is the legitimate heir (I Sam. 18.3–4). He has the support of the priests of the old sanctuary of Shiloh (I Sam. 22.20); he has received Saul's diadem and bracelet (II Sam. 1,10); and the elders of Israel have chosen him as king (II Sam. 5.3). A whole literature exalts David and makes him the prototype of the ideal king: the *māšiaḥ* (Messiah), i. e. the one who has received the royal unction – can only be a new David.

Read Isa. 9.1–6; 11.1–5; Micah 5.1–3; Pss. 2; 45; 110.

A generation later, a new redactor adds some less flattering features to this portrait. He does not hesitate to report the adultery of David, who makes an arrangement with Joab to eliminate Uriah (II Sam. 11); he shows a strange indecisiveness when confronted with the murder of Amnon and then the revolt of Absalom; finally, I Kings shows him old, sick and declining in mental powers. That is explained by the fact that the author seeks to endorse Solomon, who took power by a palace revolution: he has to show both that Solomon is his father's legitimate successor and that the Davidic monarchy must give place to something else.

The Deuteronomistic school tries to erase these unfavourable features or at least to compensate for them. David receives the kingdom because he is better than Saul (I Sam. 15.28). For example, he spares his rival when Saul is at his mercy, whereas Saul only sought to kill him (I Sam. 24); we find the same generosity towards his weary men when the booty is shared out after a victory over the Amalekites (I Sam. 30.23–24); or again towards Meribbaal, the son of Jonathan (II Sam. 9.1). David may be an adulterer and a murderer, but he hears the word of the prophets and repents (II Sam. 12.1–23). When he is on the point of death he calls on his son Solomon to observe the Law (I Kings 2.2–4). The David of the Deuteronomistic school is righteous, sensitive, generous, loyal, brave, always listening to YHWH, and that is why he can go from success to success. As David himself declares (I Kings 2.4), the monarchy would not have fallen had all the kings behaved in the same way.

The final redactor of the books of Samuel and Kings adds only a few new elements to the narrative, but they are significant. Nathan's oracle is supplemented with a prayer of David (vv.18–29) in which he says to YHWH: 'You also extend your promises to the house of your servant for a distant future' (v.19). The narrator is thinking of the community of Zion-Jerusalem, 'the city of David', which is the heir of his promises. The same redactor adds vv. 7–12 to chapter 8, in which we see David consecrating to YHWH the gold, silver and bronze acquired in his military conquests; in other words, he destines them in advance for the temple and its liturgy. Along the same lines, David pronounces a very similar prayer to Ps. 18 (II Sam. 22) and makes a short speech (II Sam. 23.1–7) which opens with these words: 'The oracle of David, the son of Jesse, the oracle of the man who was raised on high, the anointed of the God of Jacob, the sweet psalmist of Israel' (v.1). David is presented as both a prophet and a psalmist; in particular we note that towards the middle of the Persian period the singing of the psalms by the community assembled in the temple is considered as new prophecy.

The beginnings of the monarchy and the story of David are related a second time in the book of Chronicles. Saul is almost ignored: the narrator reports only his genealogy (8.3–40; 9.36–44) and his death (ch. 10). There is only one kingdom, and to speak of an Israel separated from Judah would be to legitimate in advance the claims of Samaria in the Persian period. Similarly, the Chronicler omits the elements which are unfavourable to David, like his adultery and his murders, and the rebellions of Absalom and Sheba, along with the weaknesses of his old age. On the other hand, the author introduces an enormous section into the narrative (22.2–29.20) about the preparations for the building of the temple and the establishment of its ritual and liturgical functions. As the founder of Jerusalem, David shares with Solomon the glory of having built the temple and of having given Israel its liturgy.

Read I Chron. 28.

Numerous psalms are attributed either to king David himself (Pss. 3–32; 34–41; 51–65; 68–70; 86; 101; 103; 108–110; 122; 131; 133; 138–145) or to Asaph or to the sons of Korah, singers and porters whom he instituted. By means of the liturgical song of the psalms, the community of Zion, 'the city of David' identifies itself with the old king, presenting itself as his heir. It is to this community that we owe the promises of divine aid and the eternal stability of the dynasty. This reading of the story of David shines through in particular in Pss. 89 and 132, which echo Nathan's promise (II Sam. 7.1–17). The same promises are taken up again and extended in a series of other texts from the Persian period: Isa. 55.3; Jer. 23.5–6; 33.15–16; 32.23–25; 37.24–28).

Read Pss. 89; 132; Jer. 23.5–6.

The New Testament suggests a christological interpretation of the story and figure of David. Jesus is the son of David by blood, which is why he has to be born in Bethlehem. Above all he is the new David, who brings to perfection what the first king of Jerusalem could only begin. At the centre of the Synoptic Gospels we find the confession of the faith of Peter, who recognizes in Jesus the Messiah, i.e. the king who is son of David, sent by God to save Israel. Moreover, all his preaching is put under the sign of the kingdom, of which David's work was the first realization. It was as 'king of the Jews' that Jesus was condemned to death, and this quality is underlined throughout the passion narratives. However, the royal theme has returned in a way:

pastor *par excellence*, Jesus also takes the place of the lamb led to the slaughter; if he is king, it is not to dominate but to serve to the point of giving his life.

The history of Solomon

With David his father, Solomon is the second great king of the founding era of the monarchy in Israel. Once again his history is described in long narratives (I Kings 1–11; II Chron. 1–9).

The biblical narrative

After relating the circumstances of his accession to the throne (chs. 1–2), II Kings divides the story of Solomon into two main parts. Chapters 3–10 give a flattering portrait: he receives wisdom from YHWH (ch. 3); strengthened by this gift he administers his kingdom in a prudent way, organizing both trade and the army (4.1–5.14; 9.26–10.29); above all he builds the temple with unparalleled splendour (5.15–9.25). The second part of this picture (ch. 11) is more sombre: Solomon allows himself to be led astray by his foreign wives and encourages idolatrous cults (vv.1–13); he has to confront the kings of Edom and Zobah (vv.14–25), and then the rebellion of the Ephraimite Jeroboam (vv.26–40). This heralds the break which will come about immediately after the death of the great king.

> Read I Kings 3; 8; 10–11.

The facts

The main points have already been set out on pp. 37f. We should remember that Solomon's long reign was marked by an effort to organize the country, by the creation of a brilliant administration and a professional army, a considerable development of trade and diplomacy and a policy of major works, of which the building of the temple is the culmination.

At the same time Solomon is a hard man. He establishes himself as

David's successor by force, and does not hesitate to kill off his father's chief collaborators (I Kings 2). Then, resorting voluntarily to forced labour, he forces the whole population – especially the tribes of central Palestine – to work for the prestige of the court. Needless to say, he made many enemies.

The interpretation

The biblical narrative offers three contrasting portraits of Solomon: the wise man, the liturgist and the new idolatrous pharaoh.

The historical basis of Solomon's wisdom is the creation of a body of literate officials. The scene is set by the dream at Gibeon (I Kings 3.4–15), during which the king asks for the power to take decisions which conform to the will of YHWH ('with an understanding mind to govern your people', v.9); his wisdom can only be participation in the divine wisdom. This superhuman aptitude is then illustrated by the famous episode of the judgment of Solomon (3.1–28). In the earliest narratives Solomon is thus presented as a wise man. This quality will also be emphasized in the later tradition, as in I Kings 5.9–14 or in the episode of the visit of the Queen of Sheba (I Kings 10.1–13). Progressively all the other works of wisdom would be attributed to Solomon: collections of proverbs (Prov. 10.1–22.16; 25.1–29.27) and then, much later, the Song of Songs, along with the books of Koheleth, Sirach and Wisdom. The figure of the ideal king allied the bravura of David with the wisdom of Solomon's government.

The Bible presents Solomon as the prestigious builder of the temple. It evokes the work and the planning of the building and gives them a theological interpretation. The temple is the place in which YHWH makes his name dwell, where his glory resides (8.10–12). In a long prayer (I Kings 8.22–53), Solomon presents the temple as a place where sinners turn to their God to beg for his forgiveness. However, YHWH tells him that the unfaithfulness of the Israelites will result in the destruction of the sanctuary (9.1–9); this speech was written after the destruction of the temple in 587 and gives the explanation for it.

Solomon's prodigious wealth (I Kings 1.14–29) bears witness that his success is stunning. The Deuteronomistic school attributes it to his action on behalf of the temple. It also explains why the tribes of the

North seceded on the death of the great king: influenced by his wives, Solomon had temples built for various deities (11.1–13). All this is further developed in the episode of Jeroboam's revolt (I Kings 11.26–40).

The Chronicler (II Chron. 1–9) takes up the narrative of the book of Kings, but leaves out all the shadow side of Solomon's reign: he only wants to preserve the image of Solomon as the builder of the temple, showered with divine blessings. This time there is no contrast between David and his son: the latter finishes the work of the former. Psalm 72 goes in the same direction: Solomon expresses himself as a pious king who asks of YHWH the art of governing with justice, so that the poor are delivered.

The New Testament interprets the figure of Solomon in a christological line, like that of David. 'Something greater than Solomon is here,' Jesus declares when speaking of himself (Matt. 12.42; Luke 11.31). The text is referring to the Queen of Sheba, who came from her distant land to hear the wisdom of the king of Jerusalem: Solomon was merely announcing the coming of the wise man *par excellence*, Jesus.

The two independent kingdoms

On the death of Solomon, the tribes of central Palestine regained their independence and took as their king a soldier called Jeroboam. From then on the two kingdoms lived separate lives, and the founding period of the monarchy gives place to 'ordinary' history.

The biblical narrative

I Kings reports the assembly of Shechem, at which the tribes of the old kingdom of Saul rejected the authority of Rehoboam, son of Solomon, and took Jeroboam as their new ruler (12.1–25). The new king of Israel set up golden calves at Dan and Bethel (12.26); a religious break went along with the political break.

In addition to the notes about each king, the narrator dwells at length on the actions of two prophets, Elijah (I Kings 17–19; 21;

II Kings 1–2) and Elisha (II Kings 4–8). The former is known above all for his contest with the prophets of Baal (I Kings 18) and his pilgrimage to Horeb (I Kings 19); the latter is above all a magician who performs a series of extraordinary exploits. Then comes the story of Jehu, who massacres the whole of the royal family of Israel. In particular he kills Jezebel the queen mother, who is the main instigator of the cult of Baal (II Kings 9–10). Parallel to Jehu's revolution in Israel, the narrator reports the story of Athaliah and Jehoash in the South (II Kings 11–12). The last extended narrative is of the fall of Samaria (II Kings 17). In fact the event is related in three phrases (vv.5–6), but it then becomes the object of a long commentary.

> Read I Kings 12; 17–19; 21; II Kings 4–5; 17.

The facts

There is no reason to doubt the general historical canvas presented by the books of Kings. Besides, a large part of the notes on different reigns has probably been drawn from archives. Similarly, the exploits of Elisha beyond question go back to an early tradition. That does not necessarily mean that the details of the narrative are historical.

By contrast, the story of Elijah raises problems. Thus several episodes transfer to him events which have been told about Elisha (the miracles of Zarephath, I Kings 17.8–24; cf. II Kings 4.1–37); Hagar and Abraham (Gen. 21.14–22.19; cf. I Kings 19.3b-6); Moses (the pilgrimage to Horeb, I Kings 19); or an anonymous prophet (the affair of Naboth's vineyard, I Kings 21; cf. II Kings 9.25–26). In short, we have to ask whether Elijah, whose name ('YHWH is my God') is clearly symbolic, is a historical figure whose actions have been magnified by later tradition, or whether he must be regarded as a 'theological projection'. In that case, here we would have an anticipation of Elisha interpreted as a prophet struggling against idolatry (Jehu's massacre). Uncertainty remains.

The interpretation

The history of the two independent kingdoms (from I Kings 12 to II Kings 17) is the work of the Deuteronomistic school in the sixth century; it used earlier documents. The events are interpreted in line with the theology of the exclusive covenant with YHWH. In particular the redactors wanted to explain why first Samaria and then Jerusalem suffered such a cruel fate.

The presentation of the religious work of Jeroboam I in I Kings 12.26–33 is typical here. In the tenth century the Jerusalem temple had no monopoly, and the cult organized at Bethel and Dan was certainly that of YHWH: the 'calves' (in fact young bulls) were merely the visible supports for the invisible divine presence. However, the narrator sees this cult as idolatrous, celebrated by an unauthorized clergy; the worship of the golden calf (Ex. 32) is being resumed. So the altar at Bethel is condemned by an anonymous prophet who foretells its destruction by Josiah (I Kings 13.1–10). Then comes the conclusion: 'And this thing became sin to the house of Jeroboam so as to cut it off and to destroy it from the face of the earth' (v.34; cf. also 4.7–16). Each of the kings of Israel without exception is put under the same judgment: 'He did what was evil in the sight of the Lord, and walked in the way of his father, and in his sin which he made Israel to sin' (I Kings 15.26, 34; 15.19; cf. 16.12–13, 25–26, 30–31, etc.). Most of the kings of Judah are judged in the same way. Rehoboam too 'did what was evil in the sight of YHWH' and 'provoked him to jealousy' (I Kings 14.22); all behave in a similar way apart from Asa, Jehoshaphat, Joaz, Amaziah and Azariah, and even in the reigns of these latter 'the high places were not taken away' (I Kings 15.14; 22.44; II Kings 12.4; 14.4; 15.4). All the kings of Israel betrayed YHWH to worship idols, and it is because of this sin that Samaria received a mortal blow (II Kings 17.7–18). The ruin of Samaria is itself the last warning addressed to Judah, since the people of YHWH has been reduced from ten to one (see I Kings 11.30–32). Judah would not learn its lesson; it went on behaving in the same way and ended up suffering the same fate (II Kings 17.19, 20). Thus the whole narrative is orientated on the fall of Jerusalem, which is explained by its almost constant infidelity.

The history of the prophets Elijah and Elisha can be read in the same perspective. Elijah is presented as a new Moses: he confronts the pious Ahab and Queen Jezebel, a zealot for the cult of Baal, just as Moses confronted Pharaoh (I Kings 18; 21); it is on Horeb, *the* place in the Mosaic tradition, that he meets his God at the end of a journey of forty days across the wilderness (I Kings 19). Moreover he confronts and massacres the prophets of Baal, in the service of the local rulers (I Kings 18.20–40). Elisha in his turn is the disciple who extends Elijah's mission (I Kings 19.15–17, 19–21; II Kings 2) and thus appears as a new Joshua: allied with Jehu, he contributes to the massacre of the royal house of Omri, in particular eliminating Jezebel and all those loyal to Baal (II Kings 9–10). The true prophets are the sole witnesses to the covenant with YHWH. Like Moses, their mission is to struggle against a power which has become 'pharaonic' both in its oppression of the poor (see the affair of Naboth's vineyard) and in its idolatry. Like Joshua, they must fight the pagan or paganizing populations of the country. To persecute these prophets of YHWH is to reject the covenant and to bring down the divine anger upon oneself. This presentation of history is linked to the dramas of the years 598 and 587; the rejection of the true prophets – and of Jeremiah in particular – signifies a definitive rejection of the covenant which is punished by supreme misfortune.

The narrative of the books of Kings was supplemented in the Persian periods at several points, bringing it up to date. Thus Elijah's pilgrimage has been enriched with the famous dialogue (I Kings 19.11–14, which takes up vv.9b–10) in the course of which the prophet bears witness to three violent manifestations of YHWH (the hurricane, the earthquake, the fire) followed by 'the sound of a gentle breeze' or, more literally, 'the voice of an impalpable calm'. This sequence corresponds to the anointing of the three avengers (vv.15–17), followed by the salvation of those who remain loyal to the covenant (v.18). YHWH's last word is not repression, but gentleness and the salvation of the faithful. The end of Samaria is similarly commented on by the final redactor, who emphasizes the repopulation of the city by a pagan population which will honour both YHWH and foreign gods (II Kings 17.24–41). The narrator stresses the topicality of this conduct: 'their children likewise, and their children's children – as their fathers did, so they do to this day' (v.41; cf. already v.34). This is a way of denoting the people who remained in the land in 587 and then regrouped around Samaria as a bastard population; they are semi-pagan and thus people with whom one can have no dealings.

When the Chronicler relates the same history, from the death of Solomon to the fall of Samaria (II Chron. 10–27), he significantly omits everything that concerns Israel in the North, apart from the schism (ch. 10). In his eyes the kingdom of Samaria is no longer the true Israel: furthermore the priests and levites of the North have joined the temple in Jerusalem (11.13–17). The narrative is supplemented with a speech by King Abijah against the impious Samaritans (13.4–12). The narrator notes, on the other hand, the religious reforms undertaken for Jerusalem and the temple by the kings Asa (15.1–19) and Joash (24.1–15) of Judah. Thus the memory of the royal period is put to the service of the cause defended by the Jerusalem community in the Persian period, in its conflict with the dissidents of Samaria.

From this whole period the Christian tradition has singled out above all the figure of Elijah. The book of Malachi already declared: 'Behold I will send you Elijah the prophet before the great and terrible day of the Lord comes, and he will turn the hearts of fathers to their children, and the hearts of children to their fathers, lest I come and smite the earth with a curse' (4.5–6). In the time of Jesus people were fervently expecting the return of Elijah, who had been transported to heaven in a chariot of fire (II Kings 2) and therefore had not died. He is present with Moses beside the transfigured Jesus on the mountain (Mark 9.4). Moreover Elijah is sometimes identified with John the Baptist (Matt. 11.10, 13; 17.12; etc.) and sometimes with Jesus himself as the one who is preparing for the kingdom of God (Mark 6.14–15; 8.28; Luke 9.19).

Judah, from the destruction of Samaria to the destruction of Jerusalem

After the fall of Samaria in 722, the kingdom of Judah continued to exist for around 150 years until the time when Jerusalem suffered the same fate.

The biblical narrative

In relating the history of Judah after the fall of Samaria, II Kings (chs. 18–25) dwells on two figures, Hezekiah and Josiah, both authors of exemplary religious reforms. The former benefits from divine protection during the siege of Jerusalem by Sennacherib (chs. 18–19) and is then cured miraculously of his illness (20.1–11). The latter applies, point by point, the law found in the temple (the centralization of worship in Jerusalem, the destruction of idols and pagan emblems, the celebration of Passover, 22.1–23.35); he extends his authority over the ancient kingdom of Samaria, but is defeated by Pharaoh Necho and dies in battle at Megiddo (22.29–30). Between these two glorious reigns there is the sombre era of Manasseh the idolater (21.1–18). After Josiah one misfortune succeeds another until the final fall of Jerusalem (23.31–25.21). However, the book ends on a note of hope: King Jehoiachin is taken from his prison and eats at the table of the Babylonian king.

Read II Kings 22–25.

The facts

See pp. 40–2. The miraculous deliverance of Jerusalem under Hezekiah is probably legendary.

The interpretation

Once more, the narrative is essentially the work of the Deuteronomistic school, which wants to show the perfect justice of YHWH. Why did Hezekiah benefit from the divine favour? Because 'he did what was right in the eyes of YHWH, according to all that David his ancestor had done' (II Kings 18.3; cf. 20.3); in particular he destroyed the places of pagan worship (v.4). The king listened to the word of the prophet Isaiah (19.1–7). Similarly, Josiah's success relates to his perfect faithfulness and the fact that he listened to the prophetess Huldah (22.11–20). However, the good conduct of the two kings alone cannot save Jerusalem, which is guilty of idolatry (23.26–27).

The narrator is preoccupied throughout his work with showing that the misfortune of Jerusalem is bound up with the defection of the people and its successive kings. YHWH is angry with this city, and its fate is deserved. However, the narrative does not end with the ruin of Jerusalem: the favour shown to Jehoiachin (25.27–30) is as it were the possible opening of a new future. Who knows, if the rulers of the country behave like Hezekiah and Josiah . . .

The prophets

From Genesis to the books of Kings, the biblical narrative mentions a large number of figures who are described as prophets, like Abraham (Gen. 20.7), Moses (Deut. 18.15), Nathan, Samuel and Elijah. However, from Amos, in the middle of the eighth century, onwards, prophets of quite a different type arise. Their preaching, reported in the books which bear their names, has an essential place in the history of Israel and in the biblical witness.

The biblical narrative

The Hebrew Bible distinguishes between the 'former prophets' (from Joshua to II Kings) and the 'latter prophets' (Isaiah, Jeremiah, Ezekiel and the twelve Minor Prophets). We shall be discussing the latter prophets here.

Isaiah

The book of Isaiah comprises two very different parts. The first (chs. 1–39) contains the oracles usually attributed to the eighth-century prophet. This long section itself contains four developments:

(a) *The sin and doom of Judah and Jerusalem* (chs. 1–12). In fact this collection is not homogeneous; alongside numerous speeches in which the prophet denounces the guilt of the ruler of Judah and announces national catastrophe, we find the majority of the texts which are considered messianic.

(b) *The doom of the pagan world* (chs. 13–27); chapters 24–27 are often called the 'Isaiah apocalypse'.

(c) *The triumph of Judah and Jerusalem* (chs. 28–35). This section comprises oracles of doom, which alternate with marvellous promises. Chapters 34–35 are known as the 'little Isaiah apocalypse'.

(d) Finally, chs. 36–39 relate how Isaiah intervened during the siege of Jerusalem by Sennacherib in 701; these chapters form a narrative which is almost identical with II Kings 18–20.

The second part of the book (chs. 40–66) has been called the 'Book of the Consolation of Israel' because it begins with the invitation 'Comfort, comfort my people' (40.1); it is also known as 'Deutero-Isaiah'. The tone of these chapters is very different: if the sin of Israel is still mentioned, it is in a less precise and less insistent way. The emphasis is not on punishment, but rather on YHWH's unfailing concern for his people: the whole section stands under the sign of promises of happiness. In this framework, four passages traditionally called 'servant songs' (42.1–9; 49.1–7; 50,.4–11; 52.13–53.12) are noteworthy: these poems paint the picture of a mysterious anonymous 'servant' of YHWH whose conduct is admirable and who accepts suffering and even death so that others are spared. Chapters 56–66 are often understood to be a distinct collection, which has been entitled 'Trito-Isaiah'.

The terms 'Deutero-Isaiah' and 'Trito-Isaiah' could suggest that these are two or three literary works independent of one another. However, it would be wrong to suppose that: there is only one book of Isaiah, which holds together in its own way. Chapters 1–39 are dominated by the revelation of Israel's sin and the announcement of its punishment, even if in fact the tone changes after ch. 13. The second part of the work (chs. 40–66) responds to this: since the sin has been expiated and the punishment completed, from now on YHWH will console his people (40.1–5, which responds to 1.2–20). In this perspective the theme of 'former things' and 'new things' (42.9; 41.22, etc.) refers to the time of misfortune and the perspective of happiness regained, of which the first and second parts of the book speak respectively.

Read Isa. 1–2; 5.1–7; 6; 7.1–17; 24; 40; 42.1–9; 45.1–7; 49; 51.13–53.12; 58; 66.

Jeremiah

Read Jer. 1–4; 7.1–15; 11.18–12.6; 18–20; 23–24; 26; 28; 30–31; 36; 50–51.

The book of Jeremiah is known in two quite different forms, since the LXX is about an eighth shorter than the Hebrew Massoretic text, and its plan is not the same. The best recent studies show that the LXX reflects an original Hebrew which is earlier than MT. At all events we find an arrangement similar to that of Isa. 1–39.

(a) *The sin and doom of Judah and Jerusalem* (1.1–25.13a); this collection contains several autobiographical sections in which the prophet complains about his fate, but also bears witness to pursue his mission at whatever cost (the 'confessions of Jeremiah', 11.18–12.6, etc.).

(b) *The doom of the pagan world* (25.13b-38 and chs. 46–51, following the MT numbering).

(c) *The triumph of Jerusalem* (chs. 26–35 in the MT numbering); this section is itself framed by narratives about the sufferings of Jeremiah and other material.

(d) Chapters 36–45 + 52 offer narratives about Jeremiah and his time. Chapter 52 reproduces II Kings 24.18–25.30.

Jeremiah is thought to have preached from 626 (the thirteenth year of the reign of Josiah, cf. 1.1) to 587, i.e. during the years of crisis which affected Judah increasingly deeply before the final catastrophe. The book of Jeremiah contains four types of material: poetic oracles which often have a threatening tone, as in the other prophetic books; prose oracles; prose narratives, which above all expound the sufferings endured by the prophet; and finally chs. 30–31, which stand out from the other oracles because of the promises they contain.

Ezekiel

Read Ezek. 1.1–3.21; 8–10; 16–18; 20; 28.11–19; 34; 37; 47–48.

The book of Ezekiel opens with the fantastic vision of YHWH's chariot and the sending of the prophet (1.1–3.21). Then come four parts constructed along the same lines as the previous collections:

(a) *The sin and doom of Jerusalem* (3.22–24.27). In the middle of this collection we see the glory of YHWH leaving the temple (10.18–22).
(b) *The doom of the pagan world* (chs. 25–32).
(c) *The triumph of Jerusalem* (chs. 33–39) ending with the great battle against Gog, king of Magog (chs. 38–39).
(d) *Ezekiel's 'Torah'* (chs. 40–48): an evocation of the future Jerusalem in which everything is ordered around the temple.

This work is disconcerting. In fact the prophet was among those deported to Babylon, but in his visions he is transported to Jerusalem, and Jerusalem is at the centre of all that he says. Moreover a large number of visions have features which already herald apocalyptic.

The twelve minor prophets

The fourth prophetic collection comprises the twelve 'minor' prophets. They are minor only by virtue of the size of the books which bear their names. In the order of the Hebrew Bible they are:

- *Hosea*, who speaks of the idolatry of Israel, but also of God's tenderness;
- *Joel*, with his great vision of the day of YHWH;
- *Amos*, who denounces injustice;
- *Obadiah*, the shortest book in the Bible (just one chapter), entirely focussed on the annihilation of Edom;
- *Jonah*, which tells the story of a prophet sent to Nineveh to preach conversion there; this is the only one of the 'minor' prophets which has come down to us in the form of a narrative;
- *Micah*, a prophet of Jerusalem in the tradition of Amos;
- *Nahum*, who announces the ruin of Nineveh;
- *Habakkuk*, which contains the complaints of the prophet but also oracles of mourning and a real psalm;
- *Zephaniah*, which announces the day of YHWH and ends with great promises;

- *Haggai*, the prophet who encourages the rebuilding of the temple at the beginning of the Persian period;
- *Zechariah*, a book the first part of which (chs. 1–8) alternates fantastic visions and oracles; the second part (chs. 9–14) is close to apocalyptic;
- Finally, *Malachi*, who criticizes the priests for their bad conduct and also speaks of the day of YHWH.

In the Jewish canon of the scriptures these twelve prophets form a single work, in which the perspective of the day of YHWH has a decisive place.

> Read Hos. 1–4; 11; Joel 2–3; Amos 1–2; 7–9; Jonah; Micah 1; 4.1–6.8; Nahum 1; Hab. 2; Zeph. 3; Haggai; Zech. 2–3; 8; 9; Mal. 2.17–3.24.

The facts

From its earliest days, Israel has figures called 'seers' or 'prophets' (*n^{e}bī'īm*, plural of *nābī'*). The most famous of them are Samuel, Nathan, Elijah and Elisha. Whether as individuals or in groups, they reveal the will of YHWH and announce the future; some of them are advisers to kings, and a body of prophets of this type is attached to the temple. In its diversity this first form of prophecy, which has its equivalent in neighbouring countries, falls within the framework of traditional religion.

Around 760 BCE, a certain Amos of Tekoa (south of Jerusalem) began to preach an unprecedented message at Bethel (the religious capital of the kingdom of Samaria). In the name of YHWH, whose messenger he claimed to be, he charged the nobility with an abuse of power and announced the end of the kingdom. On the political level Amos' position is that of a reformer: he does not want to abolish the institutions but to reorientate them on real service to the population. On a theological level, however, his message is revolutionary, since it presupposes the responsibility of those whom he is addressing and indicates that YHWH could direct against his own people the power that hitherto he has put at their service. This prophet is not like the others, and moreover he rejects the title of *nābī'* (Amos 7.14). To make himself understood he accompanies his words with various expressive gestures: he mimes the royal messenger, the herald, the weeping women, a visionary prophet. Whatever the point under discussion, it seems that Amos wants to open the eyes of his contemporaries to the terrible misfortune which will not fail to come upon the country unless there is a radical change in its social policy. Rejecting the old traditional fatalism, he calls on the people to realize what is happening, but also to change their mind and their conduct. Amos was rapidly expelled, since his message destabilized the country.

The whole movement of the later 'classical' prophets derives in one way or another from the preaching of Amos. Again in the land of Israel, between 760 and 722, Hosea delivered a similar message. For him, however, the most basic sin of his people was its idolatry. So Hosea appears as the first representative of what has been called a 'YHWH alone movement'. In the land of Judah, two prophets at the end of the eighth century extended Amos's ministry, namely Isaiah and Micah, both of whom denounced the injustices of which the poor were victims. Isaiah also and above all expressed the urgency of a consistent faith, in the framework of the international policy of Judah. In fact the prophet played a major role at the court of Jerusalem, in particular during the several grave crises which followed one another between 734 and 701. Impressed by his encounter with the thrice-holy God (Isa. 6), he declared that YHWH alone holds the true power and that the country could not be saved either by a policy of alliance with a great power or by a military effort. Faith alone, incarnate in a policy of withdrawal and modesty, could guarantee the future of the country. This message is condensed in Isa.7.9b to: 'If you will not believe, surely you will not be established.'

After a long silence (we have no evidence of prophetic words in the time of Manasseh) a new generation of prophets arose from the reign of Josiah to the drama of 587: Zephaniah, Nahum, Habakkuk and above all Jeremiah and Ezekiel. Jeremiah takes up the criticisms of social injustice already developed by Amos, Isaiah and Micah. Like Isaiah, he intervenes at the level of foreign policy, inviting the king to take the side of Babylon, whose irresistible power is being used by YHWH. Announcing doom, he comes up against the official prophets, and particularly Hananiah, who on the contrary delivers an optimistic message (ch. 28). Moreover, in line with Hosea he calls on them to renounce every form of idolatry. This preaching meets with the lively hostility of the king, the prophets of peace and other influential figures (19.1–20.6; 26–29; 36–43) Jeremiah barely escapes death. So he is the suffering prophet *par excellence*. The circumstances and tone of Ezekiel's message are much disputed. Does he preach in Jerusalem or in Babylon, or first in one place and then in the other? It is hard to tell. In any case, this prophet too emphasizes the sin of Jerusalem's idolatry and sees it as the cause of its misfortunes.

A new series of prophets preach at the beginning of the Persian period: the anonymous author known as 'Deutero-Isaiah', whose message is reported in Isa. 40–55*, Obadiah, Haggai. Zechariah, Malachi and probably Joel. Their preaching has nothing to do with that of the 'conversion prophets' of the royal period; they are not interested in the sin of Israel and announce only good fortune. Their ministry should be located rather along the line of the official prophets of the temple and the royal court, whose message was optimistic. The story of Jonah is legendary. Since the end of the nineteenth century numerous exegetes have felt able to claim that Isaiah 56–66 is the work of an anonymous prophet distinct from 'Deutero-Isaiah'; this hypothesis is contested today, and it is better to take this section as a written work extending the message of chs. 40–55.

As has been noted above, individual prophecy disappeared in the course of the Persian period. The essential thing, above all from Ezra on, is to understand to apply and to update the written Law, which is ceaselessly commented on. Everything has been given in the Torah; no new founding word is necessary. We can understand along these lines the formation of the literary corpus of the Nebi'im, framed by two invitations to observe the Law (cf. above, p. 62); from now on the prophets are no longer living preachers but books which extend the Torah.

In the first century of our era we see a resurgence of figures described as 'prophets', notably a certain Theudas (see Acts 5.35). They challenge the established order and announce the irruption of a new political and religious order. The Baptist movement – to which John the Baptist and, indirectly, Jesus belonged – also seems to be part of the prophetic challenge. The New Testament also mentions other prophetic figures: Zechariah (Luke 1.67–79), Simeon (Luke 2.25–35) and Anna, daughter of Phanuel (Luke 2.36–38), but also prophets who act within the Christian communities (see Acts 11.27–28; 13.1–2; 21.10–14; I Cor. 12.28–29, etc.).

The interpretation

The classical prophets are orators, not writers. They did not edit their oracles themselves, with the probable exception of Isaiah, who seems to have put down in writing his 'memorial of the Syro-Ephraimite war' (Isa. 6–8*). At all events, the formation of the prophetic books was a long and complex work, extending over several centuries.

The preaching of the conversion prophets seems to have had only a limited impact at the time. However, at least they made some disciples: thus the messages of Hosea, Isaiah and Micah derive from that of Amos in a straight line. These disciples of the prophets brought together the preaching of their masters in written collections. This work, which presupposes a deliberate or unconscious selection, already involves some interpretation.

It would be a mistake to believe that the prophetic books of the Bible merely extend the inspiration of the prophets themselves. In the time of the monarchy, for example, the collections of Isaiah's oracles were commented on in a sense which blunted their point. We might take Isa. 29 as an example. In vv.1–4 YHWH announces that he is going to lay siege to Jerusalem, to the death. This message was scandalous. Doubtless reflecting on the basis of the traditional belief in the inviolability of the Holy City, and further reinforced be the events of 701 (Jerusalem had survived a siege imposed by the Assyrian Sennacherib), a redactor soon supplemented the speech by adding vv.5–7: at the last moment YHWH will intervene in a miraculous way to save his city. It is no longer YHWH who lays siege to the city, but the 'host of all the nations' (v.7), and this is held back by YHWH. From now on there is nothing disturbing about the speech: it proclaims the intervention of the God of Israel in favour of his people, against the hostile world. This transformation of what Isaiah says does not imply any intention to betray the prophet's word; on the contrary, it shows a concern to accept this word faithfully. It would have been so simple to eliminate these verses, which seemed to contradict the Zion tradition. But the preference was to keep the text and try to find an acceptable meaning in it by integrating a new historical experience (the siege of 701). This is just one example among many of the procedures used by the redactors: we can see that they did not necessarily continue the master's thought.

It seems most probable that it was the Deuteronomistic school of the sixth century which brought together the small collections of oracles to form proper books. The books of Jeremiah, Amos, Hosea and Micah (and perhaps also that of Isaiah and others) have been edited or re-edited by two or three successive Deuteronomistic redactors. Re-editing also means re-interpreting in the light of recent events: the dramas of 598 and 587. From Amos on, the prophets had announced a terrible disaster, and no one had believed them; however, what they had said had happened! So if one re-read their oracles, one found in them the announcement of the ruin of Jerusalem. In this perspective, the prophet is no longer the man who proclaims the current catastrophic situation of his people (sin, from which misfortune can come), but rather the one who announces the future and, more precisely, the great misfortune: for this see Jer. 28.8–9 and Deut. 18.21–22. *The* prophet is Moses, preacher of the covenant: he comes to remind Israel of the demands of the Law (with the ban on idolatry at their head); however, the prophet is rejected, and this refusal to hear him seals the destiny of the people (Deut. 18.17–19). The expulsion of Amos (Amos 7.10–17) and the cruelties inflicted on Jeremiah (Jer. 24; 36.37–38) also show the obstinacy of the evil heart of Israel: since Israel did not heed the warning, YHWH sees himself forced to inflict the punishments provided for if the covenant is violated.

In the Persian period there were no more 'conversion prophets', but optimistic prophets, whose message was more in line with the traditional thought of Israel. Along this line the prophetic collections were restructured on a common plan which corresponds to a theology of history: the prophets have brought to light the sin of Jerusalem and proclaimed its doom, but then comes the doom of the pagan world, which itself announces the triumph of Judah and Jerusalem. This is the current plan of the books of Isaiah, Jeremiah (LXX) and Ezekiel. For the reader of these books, the disaster lies in the past and all that still applies is the announcement of the end of paganism and the restoration of good fortune for Jerusalem. The redactors of the Persian period add magnificent promises to each book, in particular at the end of each collection; see for example Isa. 66; Jer. 30–31; Ezek. 40–48; Amos 9.11–15. From now on prophecy expresses above all the hope of new times.

The prophetic books made a great impact on Jesus himself and on the New Testament. Jesus was certainly aware of extending the mission of the former prophets. When speaking of himself he cites the saying, 'No prophet is acceptable in his own country' (Luke 4.24), and his contemporaries were ready to consider him a prophet (Matt. 21.11, etc.). More precisely, the people of his time saw him as *the* Prophet, the new Moses (John 6.14; 7.10; cf. Deut. 18.18), Jeremiah or Elijah returned to earth (Matt. 16.14). These figures need not be contrasted: it is always the eschatological prophet who is expected in the framework of the coming of messianic times.

So Jesus was perceived by his contemporaries as a prophet of the end of time. He preached the breaking in of a new world. He did this in a different way from John the Baptist, who announced the wrath of God and the need for conversion to escape it. For Jesus, the coming of the kingdom of God is a positive event: it is the time of the divine grace, of forgiveness offered generously to sinners, of the gathering together of all Israel without distinction between clean and unclean. If Jesus demands an effort at moral conversion – in line with the classical prophets and John the Baptist – it is no longer as a condition of salvation but rather as its natural consequence.

In the Gospels, Jesus is aware of his prophetic mission. He knows that the Spirit dwells in him, sent to bear a word of revelation. This identification seemed especially important when he began to envisage a violent death. He knew that Jeremiah and so many other prophets, down to John the Baptist, had paid a high price for their free words, and that many of them had been assassinated: 'Jerusalem, Jerusalem, you kill the prophets and stone those who are sent to you . . .' (Matt. 23.37). More than once he refers to the 'servant songs' and particularly to Isa. 53: is he not pre-eminently the lamb which allows itself to be led to the slaughter when no fault is to be found in it? The New Testament sees Jesus as the one who fulfils this great text, which describes the death of the righteous man and announces that then 'he will see a posterity' and 'prolong his days' (Isa. 53.10).

7

The great trial

The time of misfortune began in 598, when Nebuchadnezzar deported the social elites of Jerusalem to Babylon. Eleven years later, after a new siege of the city, he put an end to the kingdom of Judah. This time he was no longer content with a new deportation: he burned down the temple, dismantled the walls of Jerusalem and abolished the monarchy. The population, which believed that it was protected for ever by YHWH, was stupefied. Its faith had been given a rough test. How was it still possible to believe in YHWH? Had he been defeated by Marduk, god of Babylon? Was he a wicked, violent, unjust God? These tormenting questions challenged the most deeply rooted of Israelite convictions. The responses of those who remained in Palestine differed from the responses of those who had been deported. For once, the account here will not take the usual course (biblical text, facts, interpretation), as there is hardly any developed biblical narrative relating to this period. Since the facts have been presented above (p. 43), it is necessary only to expound the interpretations offered by the Deuteronomistic and the Priestly schools.

The Deuteronomistic school

What is commonly called the 'Deuteronomistic school' brought together several authors who doubtless wrote in Palestine at the time of the exile. The essential details have already been outlined above: the Deuteronomistic editions of the Pentateuch in general, but also more specially those of Gen. 1–11, the history of the patriarchs, the history of Moses, the books of Joshua and Judges, the history of Saul and David, of Solomon and later reigns, and finally of the prophets. It is enough here to recall the main hypotheses put forward by exegetes today and to attempt a synthesis of the Deuteronomistic theology.

Current hypotheses about the Deuteronomistic school

The term 'Deuteronomistic school' is used because the book of Deuteronomy develops its theology massively, in particular in the speeches of Moses (1–11 and 27–30) which frame the code (12–26). However, we should not misunderstand what this means: the Deuteronomistic work is not a direct extension of Josiah's reform, known as the 'Deuteronomic reform', the charter of which is the code in Deut. 12–26. However, this code is included in the new synthesis, along with much other material.

This group of writers was to give Israel a vast historical synthesis extending from the beginnings of humankind to 587; this included the Pentateuch in course of development and what is known as the 'Deuteronomistic history' (the books of Joshua, Judges, Samuel and Kings). The authors of this monumental work made use of earlier documents which they arranged, completed and interpreted: the old J narrative was already supplemented with the Elohistic contribution (E), the ancient 'scroll of the Law' discovered in the temple in 622, the royal archives, etc. The same school provided a revised edition of the prophetic books: Jeremiah, Hosea, Amos, Micah, and probably Isaiah and others. The whole of the former literature was taken up and re-edited in the light of the formidable questions posed to the faith of Israel.

This enormous work took several decades, in different phases which are the object of lively discussion. To schematize, two positions dominate current research:

– Generally speaking, Anglo-Saxon exegesis distinguishes between a Deuteronomistic redaction before the exile (Dtr I), put in the time of Hezekiah or Josiah, and an exilic redaction (Dtr II). Moreover it is necessary to take account of earlier pre-Deuteronomistic writings.
– German-language exegesis prefers to distinguish between the Deuteronomistic historian (DtrH), writing immediately after 587, a redactor above all interested in prophecy (DtrP), and another redactor interested in legal questions (DtrN). These three redactors are to be put in the exilic period.

Can we speak of a Deuteronomistic school before the exile or even before Josiah? Did this school work in Palestine or in Babylonia? Did the same redactions affect the Pentateuch and the other Deuteronomistic writings? These questions are a matter of controversy. The scholars are unanimous only on one point: an important Deuteronomistic redaction tries to understand the reasons for the great disaster at the end of the period of the monarchy. We may add that a large number of texts would seem to reflect the point of view of the second generation to be struck by misfortune; this generation feels innocent of the sin which caused the misfortune and thus hopes for an imminent return of YHWH's favour. Attention is shifted from the past catastrophe and fixed on the present and the future, conditioned by the attitude of the people; these texts emphasize the need to choose the way of faithfulness to the Law (see e.g. Deut. 30.15–20).

The theology of the Deuteronomistic school

Though we have to distinguish several Deuteronomistic redactions linked to different historical situations and thus offering messages which are not identical, the different authors belong to the same current of thought. In it we can essentially recognize a common theological thought of which the covenant forms the vital centre.

The theology of the covenant (*berit*) is not a creation of the Deuteronomistic school, but that school gives it a central place and the characteristic form of a bilateral contract. The model for the covenant of YHWH with his people is provided by the practice in international relations. Above all among the Hittites, numerous treaties have been found in which two kings enter into obligations towards each other: the more powerful accords his protection to his partner, while the inferior ruler promises exclusive loyalty to his protector. In the same way the covenant between YHWH and his people is a bilateral commitment between unequal partners; in Josh. 24, for example, we can see the people choosing YHWH in complete freedom. The terms of Israel's commitment are set down in the Law entrusted to Moses (Ex. 20–23, then Deut. 12–26), and which gives a concrete application to the Decalogue (Ex. 20.2–17 = Deut. 5.6–20). Emphasis is put on the legal character of the covenant and the duties of Israel. The destruction of the kingdom of Judah and the temple then take on a precise meaning: YHWH has inflicted the punishment provided for if the covenant is broken.

Another essential idea is that of equitable retribution. Its criterion is loyalty to the covenant, i.e. the rejection of idolatry and pagan customs, and an exclusive commitment to YHWH. The whole history of Israel, and particularly the history of the period of the monarchy, is interpreted in terms of this theory. The pious kings had long and prosperous reigns; by contrast, the impious kings drew the divine anger down on their people and themselves. So YHWH is a just God who recompenses his faithful but punishes those who betray the covenant. Beyond strict justice, YHWH reveals himself as a good God who has often renounced legitimate punishment to give new opportunities to his people (see Ex. 34.6–7).

The theology of the covenant makes it possible to explain why the misfortunes of 598 and 587 could have happened. The Deuteronomists seek to respond to an accusation against YHWH, that he had not kept his promises and had betrayed Israel. In truth, it is Israel which is guilty. In the time of Moses (see the episode of the golden calf in Ex. 32) and then increasingly, Israel had rebelled against YHWH, to follow foreign gods. Hardly had the covenant been concluded when it was broken by the people, and the same treason was renewed all down history. Consequently the Deuteronomistic school opens many books with the great scene of the trial and condemnation of Israel, guilty of having broken the covenant: Isa. 1.2–20; Jer. 2.1–37; Hos. 4.1–11a; Amos 1.3–2.16; Micah 1.2–7; cf. Micah 6.1–8; Deut. 31.19–22b, 28–29; 32.1–43. Heaven and earth bear witness that YHWH's action against his people was simply justice.

The fall of Jerusalem and the rejection of Israel did not take the people by surprise, but had been announced a long time beforehand. This is what is expressed by the reflection on prophecy: the prophet is charged with announcing to Israel the misfortune which is in store, in order to lead it to conversion. The Deuteronomistic school makes the prophet no longer the spokesman of YHWH who unveils to the people the tragedy of its situation, but the one who announces an event to come, the capture of Jerusalem by Nebuchadnezzar. Israel failed to fulfil its commitments, and its repeated unfaithfulness deserved death; furthermore, it had been warned several times, but had heeded the warnings given by the prophets (Amos 2.12; 7.12; Micah 2.6–11; Isa. 10.9–11, etc.). This interest in prophecy finds an echo even in the way that the history of Israel is related: the patriarchs and the most important characters (Moses, Samuel, etc.) are all presented as prophetic figures; on the other hand, the narratives about the prophets occupy a major place in the books of Samuel and Kings. Quite apart from the prophets, YHWH in his patience has given a solemn warning to Israel: the fall of Samaria in 722. God did not want to destroy all Israel, but allowed a little tenth (= Judah) to go on existing in the hope that it would finally learn its lesson and be converted. It was lost labour: Judah sinned even more than Samaria, and so Jerusalem had to be destroyed in its turn (Isa. 6.12–13a; Amos 4.4; 5.6; II Kings 17, etc.).

This theology, which puts all the responsibility for events on the people, contributed towards restoring confidence in YHWH. The last Deuteronomistic editions were able to formulate a new hope on this basis. The covenant had been broken, and Israel was no more than one people like all the rest (Amos 9.7–8a). However, not all hope had been lost. Had not YHWH removed the sinful rulers from his people? Would not Israel thus purified rediscover its God? Rid of its corrupt elites, it would convert to the good (Isa. 1.21–26) and again experience good fortune, as at the time of the entry into the Promised Land after the long wanderings in the wilderness. In the last resort, the drama of the end of the sixth century is not a death, but an indispensable test to ensure that Israel will live truly and welcome the gift of YHWH.

The Priestly school

If the Deuteronomistic school expresses the reflection of a group of believers who remained in Palestine, there is no equivalent testimony for the people of Judah deported to Babylon. The best evidence of the interpretation of the misfortunes of the sixth century among those who were deported is indirect. It is the Priestly redaction of the Pentateuch (P), probably written after 500 in Jerusalem, by priests echoing a reflection which had matured during the exile. The redactor P has already been introduced in the framework of the formation of the Pentateuch and his interpretations of the history of origins, the patriarchs and Moses were expounded earlier.

Whereas the Deuteronomists are the spiritual heirs of the great prophets, P is situated more in line with the sacral traditional thought of Israel and the ancient Near East. Here we find the mythical perspective of an immutable and hierarchical ordering of the universe, with the classical opposition of the sacred and the profane; this latter is also emphasized at the levels of time (sabbath and religious festivals) and space (holy place). The Priestly school attaches great importance to the temple and its substitutes: Noah's ark, the burning bush, Mount Sinai, the Tent of Meeting. YHWH is the Holy One, who is separated from the world of human beings, and the function of Moses, Aaron and the priests will be that of intermediaries of mediators. The cosmic order also manifests itself in the sequence of times, hence the large number of genealogies and chronological notes. History is divided into great stages, the crisis issuing in a new covenant (the creation of the world, Gen. 1; the covenant with Noah, Gen. 9; the covenant with Abraham, Gen. 17). Correlatively, we can see a lack of interest in human freedom and ethical questions: the notions of human responsibility and guilt would seem alien to P texts.

The creation narrative (Gen. 1.1–2.3), put at the head of the narrative of origins and the whole history of Israel, forcibly expresses Priestly thought. After the title which sums it up (1.1), the narrative opens with the state of the earth before the intervention of the creator: 'The earth was without form and void, and darkness covered the abyss' (v.2). This is the image of an uninhabitable world, plunged into utter darkness, under the sign of the abyss (*t^ehom*), a word which suggests the incarnation of evil (Tiamat) in the Babylonian creation narrative. So there is chaos at the starting point of the narrative. God is going to transform this evil world by his ten creative words, which refer to the Decalogue, the Ten Words central to the Law revealed by Moses: he imposes his Law on it. The darkness is driven back: it is not suppressed, but has to give place to light, so that the world is subject to the alternation of day and night (1.3–5). The mass of the waters of death is divided (the firmament 'separates' it, 1.6–8); then it, too, is driven back to give place to dry land (1.9–10). In this framework God produces vegetable (1.11–13) and animal (1.20–25) life, and finally human life (1.26–29); thus he triumphs over death, represented by the land which was uninhabitable at the beginning. At the centre of his composition the author puts the creation of the stars (1.14–19), the function of which is to separate day and night and to illuminate the earth, but also to determine the liturgical calendar ('the festivals, the days and the years', v.14); these are the 'lights' (*m^e'orot*), like the lampstands (*M^e'orot*) of the temple, and thus the earth becomes a vast sanctuary, in which God make himself present at liturgical feasts. Finally, the author makes the seventh day the prototype of the sabbath (2.2–13), the culmination of the composition. Once again the emphasis is on the alternation between ordinary time and sacred time: moreover, the sabbath is the distinctive mark of Israel, so much so that the narrative suggests the final triumph of the Israelite community.

This narrative is promise for Israel and for the world: it is only in hope that we can say with God that everything is 'good' and even 'very good'. Everything that is to follow in the Book will merely extend the first page. The history of Israel is a history of salvation, i.e. the constant repetition of the transition from darkness (violence, oppression) to light. It is the place where God ceaselessly fights against the forces of evil (thus the separation of the waters characterizes the miracle story of the Sea in Ex. 14 and the crossing of the Jordan in Josh. 3–4). So it is not surprising to encounter misfortune, a residue of chaos: God limits its virulence, but it will disappear only at the end of time. Even the drama of 587 must neither be taken tragically nor imputed to the guilt of Israel, which P does not envisage for a moment. The most tragic events are merely transitory returns to the original darkness, while the final victory over evil and the triumph of Israel are already programmed.

The Priestly theology is resolutely optimistic. God promised Noah that he would stop any new flood from destroying the earth and making it regress to chaos (Gen. 9.13–15). Similarly, he promised Abraham that Abraham would be 'extremely fruitful' (Gen. 17.6), as he had already promised the human being in Gen. 1.28. In other words, Israel has nothing to fear: its good fortune is guaranteed, even if its present situation is difficult. This thought has analogies with that of the optimistic prophets of the beginning of the Persian period (Haggai and Zechariah), who present the building of the new temple as a new creation of the world.

8

The time of God's silence

By its violence, the crisis which broke out in 587 battered the consciousness of Israel and destroyed its faith to such a degree that it had to rework it in depth. This is evident from the works of the Deuteronomistic and Priestly schools. In its most acute phase the crisis was of relatively short duration. The Deuteronomistic preaching made it possible to make sense of the events and gradually to regain trust in YHWH. The exiles organized themselves and once more achieved a degree of prosperity. In 539 the Babylonian empire collapsed, and the Persians soon allowed the exiles to return and rebuild the temple. Would life go on as before? Many people hoped so, but they suffered disappointment after disappointment. For the Israelites experienced painful conflicts: they felt threatened, and remained subject to the power of the pagans. The acute crisis was succeeded by a time of penetrating questions: how long would this misfortune continue? Had YHWH, who remained silent and inactive, forgotten and denied his people? These questions dogged Israel, or at least the Jerusalem community, all through the Persian period. For the only point of view that has come down to us is the community of the former exiles, whose life was focussed on the temple and its customs. In this still obscure context, three figures emerge: Zerubbabel, Nehemiah and Ezra.

Zerubbabel and the second temple

The figure of Zerubbabel is linked to the rebuilding of the temple at the beginning of the Persian period; in this connection he played an important symbolic role for the Jerusalem community.

The biblical narrative

Apart from the two simple mentions of Zerubbabel at the head of a caravan of Zionists who return from Babylon to Jerusalem (Ezra 2.2; Neh. 7.), the Hebrew Bible recalls only his role in the rebuilding of the temple. This is attested in the books of Haggai and Zechariah (chs. 1–8), and also in the first part of the book of Ezra (1–6). In his eulogy of the great ancestors Ben Sirach once again recalls that Zerubbabel built the temple (Sirach 49.11–12).

> Read Ezra 1; 4–6; the book of Haggai; Zech. 1–8.

The facts

Governor of Jerusalem around 515, Zerubbabel was a grandson of Jehoiakin, the king deported to Babylon in 598. With the high priest Joshua, and supported by the prophets Haggai and Zechariah, he undertook to rebuild the temple, which had been destroyed in 587. His function as governor, his membership of the royal family and the building of the new sanctuary sparked off the hope of a return to the old order, but it was quickly dashed.

The temple

The temple built by Zerubbabel played a central role in the life of the Jewish community in the Persian period and until its destruction in AD 70.

Built by Solomon – on the foundations of a Canaanite sanctuary? – between around 966 and 959, the first temple of Jerusalem was used until its destruction in 587. Nothing of it remains, so reconstructions are hypothetical. According to the biblical text, the building measured one hundred cubits, around fifty metres long. Along its length were three successive spaces:

– The porch, a vestibule comparable to the narthex of Christian churches. In front of this porch stood two columns which could be a vestige of Canaanite steles.
– The 'holy place', a vast room (twenty metres by ten metres) deco-

rated with sculptures and illuminated by openings near the ceiling. The room contained rich furniture: a 'golden altar', the table of show-bread, ten candelabra, lampstands, and so on.
– The 'holy of holies' – forming a cube of around ten metres, plunged in darkness. This was the heart of the temple, the abode of YHWH (cf. I Kings 8.12), who was represented by the ark, itself surmounted by two cherubim of gold-plated olive wood. YHWH, 'who sits above the cherubim' (II Sam. 6.2), was enthroned invisibly there.

This building was surrounded by annexes on three levels: store rooms for the offerings, rooms for the priests, etc. The whole complex stood in the middle of a court or 'temple forecourt'. In front of the temple itself there was the altar for sacrifices and the 'bronze sea', a vast basin probably intended for the purification of the priests. The temple complex itself was set in a more important space, which comprised the royal palace.

So the temple of Solomon was burned down in 587. A second temple was built between 520 and 515, on the initiative of Zerubbabel and the priests Haggai and Zechariah. This temple remains almost unknown: it almost certainly took over the setting, plan and general dimensions of the ancient building. We can get some idea of it from the description of the ideal sanctuary in Ezra 40.1–44.9 (a text from the Persian period).

In 169 BC Antiochus IV Epiphanes pillaged the temple; two years later he introduced the cult of Zeus Olympius there; in 164 Judas Maccabaeus recaptured the city, purified the sanctuary and re-established the cult of YHWH.

The last stage of the history of the temple is marked by the work of Herod, who embarked on a great programme of beautifying it. In essentials, the work lasted for ten years (from 20/19 to 9 BC), but continued with several interruptions until AD 64. On this occasion the surface of the temple plain was doubled. This second temple restored by Herod was destroyed in AD 70, at the end of the first 'Jewish War'. All that is left is the western wall, which Christians call the 'Wailing Wall', because Jews go to pray there. In fact it is part of the walls of the outer precinct.

The festivals

In the time of the monarchy people went up on pilgrimage to the sanctuary on the main religious feasts, according to ancient Canaanite custom. The main festivals formed part of an annual cycle linked with agriculture; their main aim was to ensure the fertility of the soil.

(a) The Feast of Unleavened Bread marked the beginning of the barley harvest. For a week, people ate bread without yeast, i.e. without grain from the old harvest: this was the transition to a new year. The main rite of the feast was the offering of the first sheaf (Ex. 23.15; 34.20; Lev. 23.9–14). This agricultural festival was associated with the feast of Passover, which was of pastoral origin. Passover involved the sacrifice of a sheep, with a view to having fertile flocks; this is the typical nomadic festival, with a meal at which the animal was eaten roasted with bitter herbs (desert plants). Since the two festivals were celebrated at the same time, they were combined, later to be attached to the remembrance of the exodus from Egypt (see Ex. 12).

(b) Celebrated seven weeks after the Feast of Unleavened Bread and Passover, the Feast of Weeks or Pentecost is linked to the wheat harvest; people went up to the sanctuary to bring the deity the first fruits of the harvest in the form of two loaves made with new flour. Like the Feast of Unleavened Bread and Passover, this originally Canaanite rite was later given a strictly Israelite meaning: from then on it commemorated the covenant.

(c) The Feast of Booths is also called the 'Feast of Tabernacles'; it was celebrated at the time of the olive and grape harvest, in the autumn. Like the other festivals, it was originally an agricultural celebration, still called 'harvest festival' in Ex. 23.16 and 34.22. Its name refers to the huts of branches made in the vineyards and orchards at harvest time; later the feast was connected with the huts in which the Israelites lived during their stay in the wilderness (Lev. 23.43).

In addition to the traditional celebrations, other festivals came to enrich the liturgical calendar from the Persian and Hellenistic periods: the Day of Atonement or *yom kippur;* the Feast of Dedication,

celebrated in honour of the reopening of the temple after the profanation by Antiochus IV; and the Feast of Purim, the origin of which is
depicted in the book of Esther.

The liturgy of sacrifices

From the time of Zerubbabel, the whole life of the Jerusalem community was ordered around the temple, its ritual, its clergy and its law.
The temple was the place of incessant activity: not only the feasts but
also the daily sacrifices in the morning and the evening, and the special
sacrifices for sabbath and new moon.

The sacrificial rite which forms the heart of the liturgy could take
various forms. In the burnt offering the throat of the animal being
sacrificed was cut by the person offering it, then the priest spread the
blood around the altar, for the life belongs to God. After that he cut
up the animal and put the pieces on the altar, where it was completely
burned. This ritual, in which none of the sacrifice came to the person
offering it or to the priest, puts the emphasis on total gift, hence its
description as the 'perfect sacrifice'. However, the most usual ritual
was the 'communion sacrifice', in which the victim was shared
between YHWH (who received the fat, which was considered, like the
blood, to be the vital part, and was burned on the altar), the priest
(who received the belly and the right thigh) and the person offering the
sacrifice (who kept the rest). This time the emphasis is placed more on
communion with YHWH. Other kinds of sacrifice express the expiation of sins: the 'sacrifice for sin' and the 'peace offering'. We should
note that the priest is not the one who cuts the animal's throat but the
one who puts it on the altar, a place inaccessible to ordinary mortals.

The song of the Psalms

The temple liturgy made great use of music and singing. The repertoire
is well known: we find it in the Psalter. The Psalter was formed progressively, and small collections were little by little brought together
to form a book of 150 liturgical songs. It is difficult to determine the
age of the psalms, since they rarely refer to historical events apart from
those relating to the origins of Israel, and the literary genres used could
have been current for long periods. Just a few psalms seem to go back

to the period of the monarchy (certain royal psalms, for example); the majority of the Psalter was probably written in the Persian period or later, in the Hellenistic period. Over and above the more elaborate classifications which have long been suggested, we can distinguish three types of poems among the psalms: some are reflective without addressing God (Ps. 1, for example); others are above all prayers of supplication, which dominate the first part of the Psalter; yet others are praises, the majority of them in the second half of the book. Thus, progressively, the Psalter passes from petition to praise: that is the fundamental movement of Israelite prayer.

The Psalter is put under the authority of David; several dozen psalms are attributed to him. However, David did not compose any of them. When the Jerusalem community sang psalms which it attributed to the first king of Judah, it was presenting itself as the 'city of David', the heir of the promises made to this illustrious figure. That fits with the presentation of David as a liturgist developed by the Chronicler (see pp. 104f. above). Furthermore, when the voice of the prophets fell silent (probably during the fifth century), the song of the Psalms was considered a new prophecy. So it is that II Sam. 23.1–7 (a text written in the Persian period) puts a discourse of a prophetic type in the mouth of David, 'singer of the songs of Israel'.

> Read Pss. 8; 15–16; 22–23; 29; 42–43; 46; 48; 50–51; 63; 72; 74; 84–85; 91; 93; 95–96; 118; 123; 126–127; 130–131; 136; 137; 149–150.

The interpretation

The presence of the great temple of YHWH in Jerusalem led Israel to reflect on its meaning, in continuity with the Near Eastern traditions relating to sanctuaries.

The divine abode

YHWH exercises his sovereignty over the entire cosmos. His presence is not confined to any particular place (cf. I Kings 8.27), but it is not just anywhere: he dwells in heaven. On earth he possesses a dwelling, the temple. In Hebrew this bears the name *bayit*, 'house', or *heykal*, 'palace': it is 'the abode where YHWH dwells for ever' (I Kings 8.13).

Ezekiel described the glory of YHWH leaving the temple (Ezek. 10.18–22); this signified its imminent destruction. This presence in the sanctuary justifies the offering of sacrifices in this place, which is itself carefully isolated from profane space by a precinct, an enclosure. In fact, since YHWH dwells in his temple, in a way it touches heaven; there is an echo of this conception of the sanctuary in Jacob's exclamation as he awakens after his dream: 'How terrible is this place. It is not less than a house of God and the gate of heaven' (Gen. 28.17).

The sacred mountain, centre and microcosm

Since the temple is by definition the place where earth touches heaven, in Near Eastern religions it is associated with the symbolism of the cosmic mountain. Thus the main temple of Babylon, the E.TEMEN. AN.KI or 'House of the Foundation of Earth and Heaven', was symbolically a mountain in seven storeys, embodying the seven levels of the cosmos and allowing contact with the heavenly sphere: we can see Jacob's vision of the 'ladder', or rather 'stairway', in these terms (Gen. 28.12).

This mountain sanctuary is not only the centre of the universe, from which all life comes, and the sole point of contact between human beings and the world of the gods (*axis mundi*), but also the embodiment of the whole of the cosmic order (*imago mundi*). Along these lines, in Jerusalem the symbolism of Mount Zion was used: Ps. 48 describes the temple hill as a 'holy mountain, beautiful in elevation, the joy of all the earth' (vv.2–3). These ancient representations were extended in the period of the second temple. The construction of the new sanctuary corresponded to a shaking of the cosmos (Hag. 2.5–6). All nations travel to its light (Isa. 60; Hag. 2.7–9; Zech. 2.15) and the earth will give its produce afresh (see Hag. 1). To rebuild the temple is to recreate the world, to pass from a disorganized chaos to a cosmos ordered around its centre.

The place of divine stability

The Near Eastern traditions deliberately contrast heaven, the place of immutable stability, with earth, the scene of a change which is as constant as it is useless (see e.g. Pss. 2.1, 4). The agitation of the world below prolongs the original violence of chaos: it threatens the very structure of the cosmos established by God and thus focusses on the centre, the symbol and the embodiment of divine order, the temple mount. Hence the images of the attack of the peoples or the raging waters on the city of YHWH (Pss. 2.1–3; 46.3–4, 7, etc.). These express a fundamental disquiet: beyond the ruin of Jerusalem there is a fear of the collapse of the cosmos and a return to chaos. So these images express terror at the end of the world, as in the old story of the flood. This disquiet is met with the assurance of divine protection: YHWH cannot abandon his dwelling to the forces of evil, but assures it an eternal inviolability. That was the conviction of the people of Jerusalem in the time of Jeremiah, when they cried out, 'The temple of YHWH! The temple of YHWH! The temple of YHWH!' (Jer. 7.4), and said, 'We are safe' (v.10). Despite the catastrophe of 587 we find a similar assurance in the texts which certainly refer to the second temple. At all events, the violent assault of the peoples will give place to a peaceful ascent, to the pilgrimage of the nations who will come to pay homage to YHWH (Isa. 2.2–5; 60, etc.).

Jesus had complex relations with the temple. He went there on pilgrimage because he recognized it as the place of the divine presence *par excellence*. Moreover, it was in the temple that he burst out in an anger which has remained famous: he drove out those who bought and sold, and overturned the tables of the money-changers and the seats of those who sold doves (Mark 11.15–19 and parallels), since the sign of God's nearness offered to all had been perverted in the service of a nationalistic religion based on mercantile relations with God (sacrifices make it possible to attain eternal life). It was the men of the temple, beginning with the high priest, who condemned him to death. In the new Jerusalem of the Apocalypse there is no temple: 'The Lord, the God who is Lord of all, is its temple, and the Lamb' (21.22). It is in Jesus Christ that from now on God is present to humanity, and the existence of a temple of stone is no longer justified. I Peter speaks of the Christian community as a temple made of living stones (2.5).

Nehemiah and the theology of the 'remnant'

The second symbolic figure of the Persian period is Nehemiah, governor of Jerusalem from 445. The circles close to Nehemiah seem to have produced a literature which is both abundant and theologically very rich.

The biblical narrative

In essentials, the book of Nehemiah contains the memoirs of this figure (a narrative in the first person). It opens with news that reaches Nehemiah when he is living in Susa (in Persia): the Jerusalem community is in distress, and cannot defend itself, as the city has no walls (ch. 1). With the king's agreement, he goes to rebuild the city walls, to the great displeasure of Sanballat, governor of Samaria, Tobiah the Ammonite and Geshem the Arab (ch. 2). Threatened by the enemy, the people rebuild the walls in fifty-two days of incessant work (chs. 3–4; 6). The city is repopulated by the families of those who had once been deported (ch. 7). Chapters 8–10 pose a problem, since the first-person narrative of Nehemiah is interrupted, and it is Ezra who solemnly reads the book of the Torah, after which the Levites pronounce a long prayer of penitence and intercession and the people promise to remain faithful to the Law. We find Nehemiah's memoirs again in chs. 11–12, which end with the dedication of the walls (12.27–43). As an appendix we find another evocation of the faithfulness of Jerusalem at the time of Zerubbabel and Nehemiah (12.44–13.3) and then the history of the new reform introduced by the governor, with a view to better service of the temple and the sabbath and against mixed marriages (unions with women who are not Jewish).

> Read Neh. 1–2; 8–10.

The facts

Nehemiah's mission began in the twentieth year of Artaxerxes I, 445 (Neh. 1.1; 2.1). Sent by the Persian king, he discovered the walls of Jerusalem to be in a catastrophic state. Jerusalem was in fact a stronghold and had been a provincial capital; at any rate, Judaea could now mint coins. The city, repopulated by Jews who had once been deported to Babylon, numbered around 6,000 inhabitants. Other information in the book could transfer to Nehemiah preoccupations which were in fact those of a later date.

The time of Nehemiah was marked by very lively tensions between the Jerusalem community, made up of those who had once been deported, and a whole world outside, where we are to locate the 'people of the land', i.e. the considerable mass of Israelites who were not descendants of the exiles. The exiles were loyal to Zion and the temple, the 'people of the land' to Samaria. The confrontation between the two groups was one day to result in the Samaritan schism. Doubtless serious dissension also arose between divergent tendencies, even within the community. There is not enough evidence, and too much is open to interpretation, for us to have a really clear picture here. However, a study of the literature of the Persian period allows us to recognize a moderate tendency, around Nehemiah, and a radical tendency, the great figure in which was Ezra. The first group, which was in the majority during the fifth century, was then supplanted by the second.

Whatever may be the truth of this hypothesis, a large number of texts present the rebuilding of the city walls as a sign of forgiveness or of the divine favour: see Ps. 51.20; Isa. 49.16. These texts, which bear the stamp of the period of Nehemiah or thereabouts, are part of a group of texts with a characteristic theology. By analogy, we can put in the same setting a series of writings which are among the masterpieces of Jewish spirituality and Jewish literature. Particular mention should be made of:

(a) The *first edition of the book of Job*. The author presents two tendencies which are in confrontation within the Jewish community of Jerusalem, itself faced by external enemies (the 'wicked'). The first tendency, represented or caricatured by Job himself, can be described as 'radical'. Obviously, oppression by the wicked was felt to be scandalous: since the Jewish community was observing the Law, how could it be that YHWH was not intervening in favour of his faithful? Had he taken the side of the wicked? The moderate party – that of wisdom and faith, the author of the poem is saying – maintains its trust in YHWH, the only recourse against the wicked. Even if his silence is disconcerting, one cannot see him as an accomplice of the persecutors. This point of view is that of Job's friends, and is confirmed by God's speech (chs. 38–39). For the author of the text, Job's proud affirmation of his own right-eousness can only lead to a gratuitous accusation of God and rebellion against him, hence Job's development from his initial complaint (ch. 3) to an increasingly proud claim. Hence, too, the development in the speeches of the friends, who gradually come to think that Job is sliding into the camp of God's enemies. In claim-ing to be right before God, the radical party risks joining the camp of the impious because of its pride. Through the voice of the friends, whom he thinks to be right, the author calls on Job to abandon his lofty intransigence and resolutely to put his faith in YHWH.

> Read Job 3; 4.1–11; 5.8–16; 6.1–13, 21–30; 18; 38.1–40.5.

(b) *Some psalms* which include an acknowledgment of sin and a plea for divine forgiveness, or at least an appeal to the grace of a great faithfulness (Pss. 38; 39; 41; 51; 69; 80; 81, etc.).

(c) *The 'teaching discourses' in the book of Proverbs* (1.8–19*; 2.1–22*; 3.1–12*; 3.21–32; 4.1–9*; 4.19–17; 4.20–27), which are an invitation to mistrust the calls of the sinners and to put one's trust in YHWH. Other sections of the book come from the same milieu, like the call of Lady Wisdom, with the theme of the seven pillars of wisdom (9.1–6).

> Read Prov. 1.10–19; 3.1–10; 9.1–6.

(d) Several short works: the book of *Lamentations* (at least in part); the book of *Jonah*, which shows how much God wants the con-version of sinners, and how he can bring it about despite the opposition of the 'hard' who reject such a possibility; perhaps also the *Song of Songs*, if it is true that it hymns the privileged relations which unite YHWH and his people.

> Read Jonah; Song of Songs 2.8–3.5.

(e) A *new edition of several prophetic books*. It is probable that the school of Nehemiah gave shape to the 'great book' of Isaiah, comprising the old sections of chs. 1–39, but also the preaching of Deutero-Isaiah and various additions. The redactor sets the first word of YHWH, which denounces the sin of Israel and announces doom (1.2–20 and the whole of chs. 1–39*), against the new divine word, which promises the consolation of Jerusalem (40.1–5* and the whole of chs. 40–66). A large part of the material in Isa. 40–66 comes from this redaction, notably the first formulation of the 'servant songs' (Isa. 42.1–9*; 49.1–9a*; 50.4–10*; 52.13–53–12*) and the passages in Proto-Isaiah relating to the 'remnant' of Zion (7.21–22; 37.31–32; etc.). As well as the book of Isaiah we should note the basic text of the 'confessions' in the book of Jeremiah (11.18–19*, 21–22 + 12.4–5*; 15.10–11*, 15–19*; 17.14, 16–17; 20.7–9, 14–18) and a large part of the promises in chs. 30–31. Similarly, passages in the book of Hosea about the restoration of Israel (2.1–3, 8–9, 16–18, 21–25, 3.4–5 etc.). We must add to this list numerous passages from Ezekiel and the other minor prophets.

Read Isa. 32.1–5; 42.18–43.7; 49.13–21; 61.1–9; 65.7–14; Jer. 15.10–21; 24; Ezek. 37; Hos. 2; Micah 2.12–13; 5.6–7.

The interpretation

This literature allows us to have some idea of the preoccupations of the Jerusalem community, or rather the moderate tendency in it, during the course of the fifth century. The Jews who visited the temple and observed all the prescriptions to the letter formed a minority which felt threatened and asked itself questions about the meaning of its trials: why did YHWH abandon his faithful to such wretchedness (see Isa. 49.14)? Several themes often recur in their reflections:

The experience of suffering

The group feels increasingly in a minority in the midst of a people which has ceased to be aware of the demands of the covenant and sees itself threatened by aggressive adversaries: only a miserable 'remnant' of the great people of Israel continues to exist. However, it is from them that YHWH will reconstitute his people; however small the community, it is the 'branch of YHWH' (Isa. 4.2; cf. Zech. 4.8), which is called on to blossom.

The Jerusalem community had complex relations with 'Israel'; in some texts the two are almost identified; elsewhere there is a mission to Israel (see e.g. Isa. 49.5, 8). So it seems that without standing for all Israel, the community is aware of forming a healthy part of it, which alone deserves to bear this name fully, or to be called 'servant of YHWH' (Isa. 42.1, etc.).

Spurred on by the conviction of forming the very heart of Israel, the believers gathered around the temple are nevertheless not euphoric. On the contrary, they do not hide their sufferings: the community lives in distress, fear and tears. It is impossible to get a precise idea of the maltreatment of which the faithful are the victims, but one thing is certain: they feel threatened, persecuted. This situation is confirmed by the building of the walls, which is to meet a strong sense of insecurity (Neh. 2.11–4.17; 6.1–7.3). The motif of rebuilding the walls of Jerusalem occupies a major place in this literature: see Isa. 26.1; 27.4; 49.16–17; 51.3; 58.12; 60.10,18; 61.3; 62.6; Jer. 1.18; 30.18; 31.4, 38–40; Micah 6.11; Ps. 51.20.

The interpretation of this suffering: YHWH remains silent

The miserable fate of Jerusalem is coupled with a more internal drama. The community is still waiting for the fulfilment of the ancient promises, in particular those about the great number of Abraham's descendants (Gen. 2.12, etc.). Without admitting it to themselves to any great degree, the group of faithful is beginning to doubt YHWH and his justice. Israel repeats: 'My way is hidden from YHWH and my right escapes my God' (Isa. 40.27). Will God let his people die, or will he intervene? Is it necessary still to believe in him and to continue to strive to be faithful, exposed to the ridicule of the majority, or is it not better to renounce him, as so many others have done? In fact YHWH is the direct or indirect cause of Jerusalem's misfortunes: his attitude does not correspond to his character as 'father' of Israel (see Isa. 63.15–17a). He is like 'a deceitful brook, like waters that fail' (Jer. 15.18) and causes his people to fear (Jer. 17.17; cf. Job 23.16). The community cries out its distress, and the only response is a heavy silence (Isa.42.14; 58.3a; 64.11; Jer. 15.11). However, whatever the hesitations, faith prevails.

The reason for YHWH's silence: the sin of his people

Why does YHWH not protect his people and listen to their prayer? YHWH can only act justly, observing the rules of an equitable retribution! So the Jerusalem community must be sinful. It observes religious regulations (circumcision, the sabbath, worship) but is guilty on the level of social relations, as is said in Isa. 58.5–11 (see also Isa. 59.3–4, 13–15a; Amos 5.15; Zech. 7.9–12; 8.16–18; Lam. 3.34–36). Painful though the suffering may be, it is also a necessary transition because it is an education. Despite appearances, YHWH is acting for the well-being of his faithful. The trial that he is inflicting on them will not last long, and he knows what treatment is suitable for them (see Isa. 28.23–29). The community of the 'remnant of Israel' comes to consider that its torments have a positive meaning: it is by accepting them without rebellion (see Isa. 50.5–6; 53.7) that the sinners will return to YHWH (cf. Jer. 15.19) and Israel will be saved; they also allow it to make expiation for the sins of the whole people (see Isa. 53.3b–6).

The hope of the 'remnant': divine forgiveness and conversion

The 'remnant' of Israel is waiting for YHWH to break his silence and finally to respond to the prayer of those who implore him. That will be the end of all oppression and all threat, and thus the return to prosperity and peace. However, the hope of the group is still for its own conversion and that of the wicked: in this way Israel will again become a great people, as YHWH had promised it (Isa. 49.2–21; 54.1–3; 66.8; Hos. 2.1, etc). The emphasis is put on spiritual healing: the deaf will hear the voice of YHWH, the blind will see his mighty acts (Isa. 29.18; 30.21; 32.23). The conversion of the orthodox community – presented as the outpouring of the Spirit (Isa. 44.3, etc.) – will allow the return of the 'others' and the realization of the promises that they will be multiplied. This conversion will not be the fruit of a voluntaristic effort on the part of Zion; it will be effective only through the grace of YHWH, who will begin by forgiving his sinful people (Isa. 33.24; 43.25; 44.22; 48.8–9; Jer. 31.22, 31–34; Hos. 2.8–9, 16–18; Jonah 3.10, etc.), that is to say to bring good fortune and peace to Zion, and in particularly the security of the walls (see Ps. 51.20 etc.).

By its theology of the divine forgiveness, which comes to supplement the human lack of any capacity for conversion, by its emphasis on the unfailing love of YHWH and by other aspects, the literature of the Nehemiah school already announces – sometimes in a gripping way – what we read in the Gospels.

Ezra and the theology of 'YHWH's poor'

The third paradigmatic figure of the Persian period is another governor of Jerusalem, Ezra, whose name is linked with the promulgation of a law which was recognized officially by the Persian authorities.

The biblical narrative

The book of Ezra begins by relating the return of the first Zionists from their Babylonian captivity to Jerusalem, in the first year of Cyrus (ch. 1). The list of these Zionists, with Zerubbabel and Joshua at their head, is given in ch. 2. As soon as they arrive in Jerusalem, the former exiles begin again to offer sacrifices in the middle of the ruins of the temple, and then they set about rebuilding it (ch. 3). The 'enemies of Judah and Benjamin' then come from Samaria to offer their collaboration in this enterprise, but their offer is rejected by Zerubbabel and Joshua; furious, these enemies set about discouraging the builders (4.1–5). Since complaints are still being addressed to the Persian power under Xerxes and Artaxerxes, the work was interrupted until the second year of Darius (4.6–24). At this moment Zerubbabel and Joshua resumed work (5.1–2). The governor of Transeuphratene sent a message to king Darius, asking him to confirm the authorization given by Cyrus (5.3–17). Darius gave a favourable response (6.1–12) and so the temple could be rebuilt and solemnly inaugurated (6.13–22).

In a second part, the book of Ezra relates the mission of the man whose name it bears. In the fifth year of Artaxerxes, Ezra, 'a scribe skilled in the Law of Moses' (7.6), went up from Babylon to Jerusalem with a whole group (7.1–10). He had a commission from the king who gave him presents for the temple and authorized him to enact a Torah to be imposed on 'all the people of Transeuphratene, all those who know the Law of (his) God' (7.11–26). So Ezra gathered together his troop; it is said to be headed by the 'sons of Phineas'. After a liturgical ceremony he sets out and arrives in Jerusalem, where he places the king's gifts in the temple (7.27–8.3). Soon, however, Ezra is told that 'the people of Israel, the priests and the levites, have not broken with the peoples of the land . . . ' and have married foreign wives (9.1–2). He convenes the assembly of the Israelites, after which all those who had taken foreign wives send them back, along with the children born of these unions.

Read Ezra 7–10.

The facts

A priest and 'scribe of the Law of the God of heaven', i.e. a specialist in Jewish texts and traditions, Ezra comes to Jerusalem from Babylon in the seventh year of Artaxerxes (Ezra 7.8). The order of the book of Ezra-Nehemiah seems to indicate that this is Artaxerxes I, and that Ezra's mission therefore began in 458, shortly before that of Nehemiah. Today, however, the majority of historians prefer to put Ezra's mission in the reign of Artaxerxes II and make it begin in 398. So Ezra would come after Nehemiah.

A priest and scribe, Ezra is also a senior official of the Persian administration. He is sent as a royal commissioner responsible for resolving certain problems relating to the province of Judah. Egypt had just regained its independence and it was an urgent matter to be sure of the loyalty of the frontier provinces. Ezra's task is spelt out in the edict of Artaxerxes reproduced in Ezra 7.12–16: the Jewish community of Jerusalem will be reinforced by volunteers who want to emigrate there from Babylon (v.13); loyalty to the Persian government will be encouraged by the sending of gold, silver and cultic objects for the temple (vv.15–24); the Law of YHWH will be promoted to the

status of a royal law (vv.25–26). Ezra is ordered to appoint scribes and
judges (v.25), i.e. officials concerned with the interpretation and
application of the Law. Unfortunately it is impossible to identify with
certainty the content of the Law promulgated by Ezra. The majority
of exegetes think that it was the Pentateuch in a provisional form or in
its present form; that is probable, since it took seven days to read and
comment on the text (Neh. 8.1–18). Be this as it may, the later Jewish
tradition saw Ezra as a second Moses, who rediscovered the Torah
and put the final touches to it.

Charged by the Persian authorities with ensuring the loyalty of the
province of Judaea, Ezra took measures favourable to the temple and
the Jerusalem community, including its most radical elements. A series
of texts which certainly go back to the end of the fifth century and the
course of the fourth show the increase of a radical tendency within the
community and express preoccupations comparable to those of Ezra
(respect for the sabbath, the prohibition of mixed marriages, etc.).
Here is a brief list of this literature to be attributed to the 'Ezra school':

(a) *The final redaction of the Pentateuch.* Several additions must be
     connected with the ban on mixed marriages (Gen. 25.23; 26.34–
     35; 27.46; 28.1–9): in Ex. 6.13–25, the genealogy of Aaron – the
     figure of the high priest – makes him the grandfather of Phineas,
     who distinguishes himself by killing an Israelite and a Moabite
     engaged in sexual intercourse (Num. 25). This same redaction
     introduced the 'Holiness Code' into Lev. 11–15, with its empha-
     sis on the obligation to separate clean and unclean.

(b) The books of *Chronicles,* to which were probably added those of
     Ezra and Neh. 8 (or 8–10) in a second edition.

Read II Chron. 15; 29–31.

(c) The *book of Job reinterpreted* by a series of additions. Job, who
     represents the radical part of the community and considers himself
     to be just, is truly innocent; on the contrary, it is his moderate
     friends who are guilty (see e.g. 42.7–10). Moreover, the blasphe-
     mous statements of Job are neutralized by others in which he
     shows humility and praises God. The author identifies with Job,

not because of his revolt but because he is the figure of the poor *par excellence*.

> Read Job 1.1–2.10 (everything that emphasizes the faithfulness of Job comes from the school of Ezra); 19,23–29; 28; 42.7–9.

(d) A large number of *Psalms*, in particular those which contrast the 'just' and the 'impious', call for divine vengeance on persecutors or emphasize the innocence of the psalmist.

> Read Psalms 26 and 139.

(e) Important *additions to the book of Proverbs*, notably the speeches of divine Wisdom (1.20–33 and 8.1–36*) and a series of sentences contrasting the 'righteous' and the 'wicked' or the 'impious' (10.3, 5, 7, 11, etc.).

> Read Prov. 1.20–33; 8.1–36.

(f) A new and long series of *additions to all the prophetic books*. Among the best known of these are the account of the call of Jeremiah (Jer. 1.4–10) by which the community identifies itself with the persecuted prophet, or the hymnic doxologies in the book of Amos (4.13; 5.8–9; 9.5–6).

> Read Isa. 41.15–20; 63.1–6; Jer. 12.1–6; Amos 5.8–9; Obadiah; Nahum 1.2–8.

The interpretation

This collection of texts does not form a unified whole, and it is not always easy to distinguish it from the texts coming from the school of Nehemiah, since there is continuity on a series of important points. For example, we find the same preoccupation with the cult, the same complaints about the wretched state of the community, and the same tension with an ardently expected salvation. However, some accents shift: the misfortune no longer leads to self-accusation and the desire for conversion, but to the impatient expectation of the day of revenge.

The suffering of the 'poor'

Those speaking here call themselves 'poor'. Before indicating an active attitude, a choice of life-style and a certain relationship with God, this affirmation expresses a passivity: the 'poor' are persecuted, victims, people who are humiliated and at bay. Several terms are used: *'āniyyīm*, 'unfortunate, oppressed'; *dallīm*, 'meagre, puny'; *'ebyōnīm*, 'wretched, beggars'; *'anāwīm*, 'miserable, poor'. This is the condition of Job, who can do no more and is abandoned by all, or of numerous psalmists who cry out their extreme distress: they see themselves within a hair's breadth of dying under the blows of their adversaries (Ps. 3.3; 6.7–9, etc). The pious community feels that it has been seized by the throat; the pressure of its enemies becomes such that it ends up thinking of nothing else. As with the 'remnant' of Israel, this suffering is coupled with a sorrowful question about God: why does God allow such a situation? Why does he not renew his saving work on behalf of his oppressed people (Hab. 1.2–4; Ps. 22.5–6; 77.11–12; etc.)? The cry of the sufferer dominates all this literature; it bears witness to the experience of those who no longer have any human hope and can only cry for help to God.

The innocence of the 'poor'

The experience of the poverty and silence of YHWH before the scandal of evil is an extension of that of the 'remnant' of Israel. However, whereas the latter read in it the mark of their own sin and a punitive education aimed at their conversion, the 'poor' will not admit this in any way; only the 'impious' can be described as sinners. They present themselves without qualification as 'the righteous nation which keeps faith' (Isa. 26.2). Any penitential sense seems to have disappeared, and the society contrasts the innocent (*ṣaddīq*), whose way is straight, with the wicked (*rāšā'*), whose actions are evil. Whereas the rectitude of the just is taken for granted, we do not find a strong enough word to describe the enemy: they are 'impious', 'violent', 'malefactors', 'assassins', 'traitors', 'fools', etc. Who are these wicked? The group is not confronting the whole of humanity. Its concrete enemies are not pagans, but rather the Israelites whom it judges to be deviants, who seem to it to have abandoned YHWH to give themselves over to paganism, i.e. especially those who appeal to

Samaria rather than Jerusalem. The orthodox community identifies itself with the people of YHWH. By contrast, the impious enemies of the community are regarded as pagans. For example, the Chronicler insists on the need for a total break with the 'peoples of the land', i.e. with the 'Canaanites, the Hittites, the Perizzites, the Jebusites, the Ammonites, the Moabites, the Egyptians and the Amorites' (Ezra 9.1; cf. Neh. 10.29). Several of these peoples had disappeared long ago: the 'Canaanites' of this period are renegade Israelites. In the prophetic books the condemnations of the foreign people are understood to be aimed at wicked neighbours and not distant or unknown populations. The main fault of these peoples is their desire to depart from YHWH, to enact their own law: to all appearances they are pagans who incarnate the spirit of evil. For them it is no longer a matter of conversion. The first duty of the Jew is to avoid their company (Ps. 26.4–5; 139, etc.).

The awaited return

The faithful community feels poor, humiliated, threatened with death, while its paganized enemies are powerful and do not seem to have any concern (Ps. 73.4–12; Job 21.7–33; Jer. 12.1–2, etc.). It is the world turned upside down. The hope of the 'poor' is that this scandal will come to an end and the natural order of the world be re-established. They do not expect this restoration from a conversion; the faithful who form the 'righteous nation' have no reason to convert; as for their enemies, they belong to the empire of evil, and so their return to YHWH is out of the question. Every perspective of reconciliation has been removed; the break is complete, without either hope or desire for return. What the community awaits, on the contrary, is YHWH's brilliant victory over the persecutors, the brutal reversal of the situation of domination (see e.g. Pss. 52 and 58, or Isa. 26.1–6; 65.13–15a). It aspires to a salvation which will come only from God and will include the merciless punishment of the torturers. This expectation is manifest, and is often expressed in the form of an unconditional divine promise: it will be the victory over the enemy and the regaining of security (see Isa. 14.30).

The temple, centre of all life

Apart from its conflict with the wicked, the main centre of interest for the group is the temple: the conflict itself for the most part relates to participation in worship. Worship occupies a disproportionate space in the preoccupations of the community, as is evident, e.g., from Lev. 1–7. So it is not surprising to discover in the literature of the 'poor' the symbolism used by the old ideology of Zion, with the same image of the assault of the forces of evil on the temple mount, the centre of the cosmos (see e.g. Ps. 93). In this context, Zion is the place of refuge, the safe haven where the persecuted faithful find their sole security (Ps. 15; 27.5; 84.4; 91.1–4, etc.). It is from the holy place that YHWH will show his power and gain the victory over his enemies (Pss. 9.4–9; 20.2–3; 76.2–4, etc.). Ezra's reform, which ended up in the triumph of Jerusalem, could appear as YHWH's response to the aspirations of the community: some texts could have been written at this privileged moment.

A 'messianic' and hierarchical community

The literature of the 'poor' gives a very important place to David as the one who organized worship and to Solomon as the builder of the temple – to the point of markedly idealizing them. The community is identified with David and his descendants, and the term *māšiāh*, 'anointed one', which in principle denotes the king consecrated by YHWH, is used in a collective sense of the group of faithful (Ps. 28.8; 84.10; Hab. 3.13, etc.). The entire community under YHWH the king is presented as 'descendants of David'; it pursues the work and destiny of its ancestor, both by scrupulous work on the cultic law and by the battle that it wages against enemies who are both numerous and powerful. This process of identification does not prevent the development of a sense of order and hierarchy within the group; this is attested for example in I Chron.5.27–6.66 and 23–27: the temple personnel – with, in order of importance, the levites, the priests, the singers, the porters, and subordinate personnel – form the vital centre of the community and enjoy great prestige, which explains the emphasis on the figure of Aaron. The role of each is fixed in detail. The emphasis is on the distinction between the various categories and their hierarchy, without making the monarchical power of the high priest conspicuous: the king of Israel is none other than YHWH.

9

The challenge of the new culture

After two centuries of Persian power, in 333 the region of Syria–Palestine swung over to the Hellenistic world. Greek language, thought and customs spread from Egypt to Asia Minor, through Syria and Palestine, adapting themselves to characteristics of each population. The Jewish communities did not escape this complex phenomenon, and the Jerusalem community itself was affected by it from the third century on. Here Judaism was confronted with a brilliant and victorious civilization which was alien to it. This was the major challenge with which the believing community was confronted from now on. How was it going to react? The Bible includes four characteristic witnesses with different attitudes: Koheleth, Sirach, Daniel and the Wisdom of Solomon.

Koheleth or Ecclesiastes

Koheleth is presented as a collection of reflections on life, death, work and other features of human life. The work is attributed to Solomon (1.1), but there is no historical foundation to this: the attribution is meant above all to give the book the authority of the wise man *par excellence*. It was composed in the third century, when Hellenistic culture was really beginning to affect Jerusalem. The book of Koheleth in fact bears the stamp of this culture; it puts the emphasis on the individual, as opposed to the impersonal anonymity which characterizes the traditional wisdom of Israel; it criticizes the Israelite doctrine of retribution in the name of experience (see 4.1–3; 8.14; 9.3, 11); it presents death as the fate promised to all human beings, no matter what their life has been (2.16; 3.19–21). Faced with such a fate it commends resignation and flight, either into forgetfulness (5.19) or into the immediate enjoyment of the small pleasures of earthly existence (2.24; 3.12; 6.17; 8.15; 9.7–10). In these features Koheleth shows analogies to various Greek thinkers (Heraclitus, Hesiod, Theognis of Megara, Monimus, etc.). Without adopting a specific philosophical system it fits the Hellenistic mentality well.

Koheleth is steeped in Greek culture. At the same time it stands apart from the Israelite traditions. The book is characterized by an absence of references to the history of Israel, to the God of the covenant and the worship which is offered to him; if it mentions the Law, it does so in a marginal way by relativizing it, like many other things (7.16–17). Above all, Koheleth expresses a devastating scepticism about several fundamental 'dogmas' of the Judaism of its time: merits and divine retribution, a positive sense of history, or even the need for asceticism. This criticism is expressed in the bitter statement which frames the book: 'Vanity of vanities, says the preacher, vanity of vanities, all is vanity' (1.2; 12.8), marked by a kind of refrain: '[All] that is vanity and striving after wind' (2.11, 17; 4.4, 16; 6..9). The absence of meaning is radical: it affects the existence of every human being, even the richest, the wisest, the most glorious, like Solomon. The scepticism of Koheleth affects all false securities, all ideologies. In particular he attacks the optimistic wisdom which claims to understand the world and fix the laws of success. Nothing escapes his biting irony, whether it be enjoyment, love, wealth, power or work. Everything is only 'vanity and striving after wind'. Religion itself comes under the same judgment; one can only approach God in humility, recognizing one's own ignorance.

On the other hand, Koheleth celebrates the joy of living: 'Light is sweet, and it is pleasant for the eyes to behold the sun' (11.7). The very fact of living, the 'act' of living, is a good which has its price, and 'a living dog is better than a dead lion' (9.4).The most ordinary everyday life is the place of happiness. Here the author is combating an ascetic spirituality which mistrusts the world and its pleasures. The realities which have been denounced as deceitful are the very ones in which one can discover the hidden treasure of 'living'. Ambition or fear of the morrow must not get in the way of living today. 'Whatever your hand finds to do, do it with all your might' (9.10); in other words, take the risk of living, of doing things. We have only one life, and no one knows what the morrow will bring; there is a time of life and a time of death, but God alone holds the secret (3.1–11). So let us live today the time that falls to our lot, says Koheleth; do not waste the present moment in vain pretensions.

Koheleth's thought might appear secular. He constantly speaks of what happens 'under the sun' or 'under heaven'. He writes as a philosopher more than as a theologian. However, his reflection is that of a believer. For him, the happiness of living is a gift of God (2.24–26; 3.13; 5.17–18; 6.1; 8.5; 9.9), as creator (see 12.1) and master of everything (3.11). Koheleth criticizes the Judaism of his time, but he has not denied his faith. Rather, he is at the join between two worlds. This position between the two drives him to a way of thinking which does not fear paradox, to the point of appearing hesitant or contradictory. Finally, Koheleth is a free man who does a real service to the faith of Israel by pushing the criticism of idols a great way. He is no more the slave of a new philosophical system than he is of his own tradition. He is a believer who discovers at the same time both the savours of a life received from the creator and the illusions of all ideologies. Even if the place of the Law in his thought may be open to discussion, he is careful not to scorn it. However, one has the impression that traditional Jewish thought – that of the God of the promise and the covenant – has become alien to him; it no longer feeds the essentials of his reflection. The new culture becomes more internalized than the old; if he takes a step further, Koheleth will abandon the faith of his ancestors, like so many Jewish intellectuals seduced by Hellenism. However, he has not gone that far; he remains on the frontier, in that dangerous zone which the believer has to explore despite everything, without cutting himself off from the world.

This subversive book has been accepted into the Jewish and Christian canon of scripture! This reception, which moreover took place only after passionate discussions, affects our understanding of the whole Bible; it can no longer be read with the naivety of first impressions.

Read Koh. 1–3; 9.1–12.

Sirach or Ecclesiasticus

Whereas Koheleth is open to Greek civilization to the point of being critical of its own tradition, Sirach takes the opposite approach. Written in Jerusalem, the work can be dated to the years 200–175, when Judaea had recently passed from the rule of the Lagids of Egypt to that of the Seleucids of Syria. This was a happy period: Seleucus recompensed the Judaeans who had helped him to defeat Ptolemy V by granting them a reduction of taxation, a restoration of the temple and much religious autonomy.

In his prologue, the Greek translator explains that Sirach wrote 'something pertaining to instruction and wisdom, in order that, by becoming conversant with this also, those who love learning should make even greater progress in living according to the law'. In other words, we have here a collection of moral teaching inviting the reader to behave in keeping with wisdom. Various themes are touched on. We find questions linked to daily life and individual experience, as in the other wisdom collections, but also an evocation of the history of Israel (44.1–49.16). Advice and reflections follow one another, as if the author had brought together a series of pieces of material without attempting to put them in a particular order. The reader has to be impressed by the recurrence of passages about the fear of God and wisdom. Furthermore, the whole work is framed by two long reflections on wisdom (1.1–30; 51.13–30), while at the centre is a discourse by wisdom personified (ch. 24).

Read Sirach 1; 4.1–10; 9; 18.1–14; 24; 44–50.

Why did Sirach write his work? To give good advice? That explanation is insufficient, since it does not take account of the polemical character of a number of passages. What is the meaning of his emphasis on wisdom, the principle, fullness and crown of which is the fear of God (1.14, 16, 18) and which is identified with the Torah (24.23; cf. 51.19)? Why does he begin his book by proclaiming that 'all wisdom comes from the Lord' (1.1)? With these affirmations the author is responding to the claims of another wisdom, that put forward by Greek philosophy and the Hellenized Jews. He himself is not insensitive to it, and scholars have thought that they could see traces of Stoicism in his thought. But if he does not escape the influence of the rising culture, he sees it as a mortal danger for the Jewish tradition. Hellenism presents itself as a superior wisdom, which mobilizes all the resources of the mind and critical spirit. Whatever its prestige, however, Greek faith destroys faith (see Koheleth as an example) and dissuades people from the traditional customs of Israel. So it is harmful: 'There is a cleverness which is abominable' (19.23). This practical intelligence rests on human effort, while human beings are only 'dust and ashes' (17.32). In truth, 'there is only One who is wise, greatly to be feared, sitting on his throne: the Lord himself' (1.8–9). The pseudo-wisdoms are mere folly, a mortal illusion.

Epicureanism, very popular in the circles won over to Hellenism, argued that the universe is the plaything of chance and denied the existence of any kind of order in the world. Sirach replies by emphasizing the idea of creation. The whole cosmos is ruled by an admirable order, established by YHWH (42.15–43.33); it is 'according to his order' that the stars shine in the sky (43.16); it is 'by his order' that God makes the snow fall (43.13); 'according to his plan' that he tamed the abyss (43.16; cf. 39.17–18). Human beings scarcely discern the fine harmony of the creation, and yet everything – even the scourges – has an indispensable function in it: 'everything has been created for an end' (39.21; this idea is developed from v.12 to v.35). The sensible man can only prostrate himself and proclaim: 'How marvellous is the work of the Most High' (34.2). It is by his wisdom, the first of his works (see 1.4), that YHWH created the universe (42.21). The divine wisdom can thus claim to have been active throughout space (24.3–6); for all that, it is fixed in Zion, the place from which from now on it shines forth (24.10–17). It is none other than the law published by Moses (24.23). One becomes wise by meditating on this law and the tradition of Israel, and by prayer (39.1–11).

The Stoics were concerned to live in unison with the pulse of the world. Ben Sirach declares that it is by observing the Law, by being concerned to do the will of YHWH, that human beings can take their place in the harmony of the cosmos and live to its rhythm. Now fear of God and observance of the commandments are necessary for all human beings (1.11–20; 10.19–25, etc.). The true wise man is not the one who follows the way of the intellectual world or tries to reflect in a critical spirit on his human experience, but the one who listens to the Torah and lives humbly in conformity with it. This is a way followed by the great ancestors who, from Enoch to Nehemiah (44.1–49.16), remained 'faithful to the commandments' (44.12) and 'observed the law of the Most High' (44.20; cf. 45.5, 17; 46.14). Judaism has become a religion of the book: wisdom is given by YHWH, with all the developments necessary to life, and there is no need to seek it by an effort of human reflection.

The fear of YHWH, the only wisdom worthy of the name, is a precious treasure (1.17; 23.27; 24.19–22; 25.11; 51.28) and the whole book calls on its readers to lead a life in conformity with the Law. This programme contains a warning: it is necessary to arm oneself against the influence of the 'lawless' (9.11–13; cf. 11.29–34; 13.1–23; 22.13) and to choose true friends, 'to seek out intelligent men' and speak with them of 'the Law of the Most High' (9.14–16). Those who want to live with wisdom must reject what comes from paganism. They must adopt an attitude of active resistance, following the example of the great believers of the past: Phinehas, who held firm 'with noble courage' when the people rebelled (v.23); Joshua, who firmly led the battles of the Lord (46.3); Caleb, who opposed the multitude and prevented the people from sinning (46.7); Samuel, who invoked the Lord when enemies were pressing him on every side (46.16); David, who brought low the arrogance of the giant Goliath (47.4); Elijah, 'who brought kings down to destitution and famous men from their beds' (48.6); Hezekiah, who fortified his city (48.17); Nehemiah, who rebuilt the walls of Jerusalem, setting up gates and bars (49.3); and finally Simon, son of Onias, who fortified the sanctuary and the city (50.2, 4).

Sirach gives a whole series of recommendations on the way to behave socially (alms, hospitality, educating children, self-control, patience, temperance, prudence, discretion, etc.). Most of his advice is merely an extension of the old wisdom reflections, but it no longer has the same foundation: the criteria of the conduct to be promoted is not so much experience as tradition, conformity with the customs inherited from previous generations. The essential thing is to safeguard the practice of traditional Judaism.

The theology of Sirach is not isolated. We find the same perspectives in an important body of literature:

(a) The book of *Tobit,* also written around 200, shows the same concern to edify its readers and exhort them to practise the Torah. The author relates how God heard the prayer of two people who were both faithful to the Law and tried by misfortune. In Nineveh, the aged Tobit, whose piety and concern for others approaches heroism, has become blind. At Ecbatana, in Media, Sarah is desperate, because her seven successive husbands have all been killed by the demon Asmodaeus even before their wedding nights. Raphael, the angel of God, comes to their aid. He accompanies Tobias, son of Tobit, to Media, and has him marry Sarah, protecting him against Asmodaeus; on their return to Nineveh he gives Tobias an ointment which enables his father to recover his sight. The book thus shows how the one who observes the Law and trusts in YHWH finally ends up receiving good fortune from him.

Read Tobit 5–6; 12–13.

(b) We may attribute the essentials of the book of *Nehemiah* and the final redaction of the *Chronistic history* to the same school. In fact the work of the Chronicler was supplemented in the Hellenistic period with a series of lists (e.g. I Chron. 2.18–4.23), but also by the greater part of the book of Nehemiah. Once again, the redactor seems to want to put the Jewish community on guard against the temptations of Hellenism. This explains why he lays so much emphasis on Tobiah the Ammonite as the main adversary of the faithful community (Neh. 2.10, 19; 3.35; 4.1, etc.); the family of the Tobiads was the figurehead of Hellenism in Jerusalem from the end of the third century on. The second mortal enemy of Jerusalem is Sanballat, governor of Samaria (3.33–34); the author doubtless has in view here the schismatic Samaritans, also detested by Sirach (50.25–26). In its present tone the book of Nehemiah is dominated by a concern to promote the observance of the Torah (1.5, 7, 9; 9.13–14, etc.), the fear of God (1.11; 5.9, 15; 7.2), the rejection of sin (1.6; 6.13; 9.2–3), solidarity between brothers

(5.10–13, 17–18) and respect for the sabbath (10.32; 13.15–22), etc.

> Read Neh. 3–7.

(c) The central sections of the book of *Baruch* present important similarities to Ben Sirach and his thought. We can recognize two independent pieces in them: a national confession of sins (1.15aβ–3.8) and an exhortation to observe wisdom (3.9–4.4), close to Sirach 24. The author of the work, who seems to be writing in Greek right at the beginning of the Christian era, made use of these pieces, which he framed with his own reflection.

> Read Baruch 3.9–4.4.

(d) Around the same period, the book of *Job* seems to have been given its definitive form, by the introduction of new developments; several passages from the speeches of the friends in which they emphasize the culpability of Job and the insignificance of human beings (4.12–5.1; 11.4–6, 11–12; 15.14–16; 22.2–11, 29–30), Job's own reflections on the great price of wisdom, which is equivalent to the fear of YHWH (28.7–8, 15–20, 22–28), the speeches of Elihu (chs. 32–37) and the second speech of YHWH (40.6–41.26), itself followed by Job's second retractation (42.1–6). Thus reconfigured, the book condemns Job and his vain pretensions, who in the eyes of the redactor represents Hellenistic culture and its prestige.

> Read Job 22.2–11; 28.15–20; 32–33; 40.25–42.6.

(e) Similarly, the school of Sirach finished the redaction of the book of *Proverbs*, introducing into it in particular the warnings against the seductions of the foreign woman – a symbol of Hellenism (2.16–19; 5.1–20; 6.20–7.27) – and the famous poem on the perfect woman, who symbolizes true wisdom, i.e. fidelity to the Torah (31.10–13).

> Read Prov. 5.1–20; 31.10–31.

(f) Finally, the *Psalter* was re-read and also completed with some anti-Hellenistic polemic. Among the numerous psalms which were probably written in this context one might mention those in praise of the Law (Pss. 1; 19; 25; 119). Put at the beginning of the collection, Psalm 1 gives the whole book its tone; in this way it becomes a collection of wisdom celebrating the good fortune of the man who is faithful to the Torah.

Read Pss. 1; 19; 103–104; 112.

By comparison with Koheleth, Sirach and his school reacted to the challenge of the new culture in the opposite direction: they regarded the seductions of Hellenism as mortal blows to the integrity of Judaism, and their prime concern was to summon their contemporaries to preserve the heritage of the ancestral tradition of Israel.

We should note that the book of *Ruth* could have been written around the same time as Sirach, but in reaction to its mentality, which was thought to be too closed. The book tells the attractive story of two women, Naomi and her Moabite daughter-in-law called Ruth. Naomi, whose name means 'My sweetness', has become Mara, 'bitter' (1.20), since she is a widow; her two sons are dead and she has no descendants. She represents faithful Israel, which feels sterile, without a future. The book relates how Naomi finds the descendants to which she aspires: through the Moabite woman, who marries Boaz. This marriage, censured by intransigent Judaism, is possible thanks to the levirate law, preferred to that which condemns mixed marriages. From their union is born Jesse, who is the father of king David. The work is not opposed to the Law, but it proposes an open interpretation: its first principle cannot be the exclusion of uncleanness (see Neh. 13) but the promotion of human life.

Read the book of Ruth.

Daniel

In the years 167 to 164, Israel experienced a dramatic crisis: the persecution by Antiochus IV Epiphanes. The confrontation between Hellenism and Judaism reached its climax: the Syrian authorities and the Hellenized Judaeans punished with death those who remained faithful to the traditional customs of Jewish religion. They burned the scrolls of the Torah, enforced participation in pagan sacrifices and dedicated the temple to the cult of Zeus Olympius. While the blood of the martyrs flowed, armed resistance was organized under the authority of Mattathias the Hasmonean and then his son Judas Maccabaeus. These events, which are described in the books of Maccabees, are evoked with precision in Dan. 11.30–39, but the author does not yet know the deliverance of Jerusalem and the purification of the temple (December 164); he can only announce the end of the persecutor in conventional terms (11.40–12.3). That allows us to put the final redaction of the book at the beginning or in the middle of 164. The redactor is probably a member of the group of Hassidim, who joined the resistance organized by Mattathias and Judas Maccabaeus (I Macc. 2.42), though without accepting their policy (I Macc. 7.13). The Hassidim were characterized by their devotion to the Torah and in particular to the cult. Dan. 11.33, 35 calls them 'the learned among the people', those who teach the multitude and figure among the victims of the persecutions.

Read I Macc. 1–4; II Macc. 7.

The books of Maccabees, which in part run in parallel, relate the history of the great persecution and the events which followed. I Maccabees, written around 100 BC, is the chronicle of the struggle against the Hellenization of the country up to the death of Simon (in 134). II Maccabees would seem to be slightly earlier; written for the Jewish community of Alexandria. It is interested above all in the fate of the temple, desecrated then purified; it is important for its advances in theology (the resurrection of the dead and prayer for the dead, creation from nothing . . .) The narrative stops at the death of Nicanor, around 160 BC.

Outside the additions in Greek (chs. 13 and 14), the books of Daniel comprise two parts of almost equal length (we should note the use of

Hebrew, but also Aramaic in 2.4b–7.28). Chapters 1–6 contain a series of edifying narratives about a certain Daniel, a young Israelite living at the court of Nebuchadnezzar; then chs. 7–12 report a series of visions of Daniel himself. These two parts of the book logically link together: since Daniel has shown that he is a man who can perceive divine messages and interpret them precisely (chs. 1–6), the revelations in chs. 7–12 must be believed in. The edifying narratives in chs. 1–6, some of which seem to have been related before the persecution, stand out here. They encourage resistance to the laws of Hellenization, even at the price of martyrdom, and announce the final victory of the God of Israel. The visions and revelations of the apocalyptic part of the book (chs. 7–12) give the same message: the concern is always to sustain the hope of the victims of Antiochus' persecution by announcing the imminent and decisive intervention of God himself, the defeat of the power of evil and the triumph of the faithful.

Read Dan. 1–2; 6–7; 11.40–12.12.

In some respects the book of Daniel extends the approach of Sirach. It in turn ridicules pagan wisdom, for example when it shows the wise men and sages incapable of telling Nebuchadnezzar the content of his dreams (2.1–13; 4.3–4, 15) or Belshazzar the meaning of the writing on the wall (5.7–8). It relates the conversion of the pagan king, who recognizes the God of Daniel and his companions (2.46–47; 3.28–29; 4.34; 6.27–28). Similarly, the book offers as models those who refuse to transgress the Law, no matter what the cost: Daniel and his friends who will not eat unclean food (ch. 1), the three young people who do not prostate themselves before the effigy of the king (ch. 3), Daniel who continues to pray to his God (ch. 6). By all accounts the aim of the work is to encourage believers to remain faithful to the Law, even if they have to pay for that with their lives. Divine retribution is bound up with this attitude: Nebuchadnezzar could escape death if he agreed to stop sinning (4.24), But the desecration of the sacred vessels and violence towards the faithful draws down the divine condemnation (5.26–28, 30); on the other hand, the victims of the repression will rise again (12.2–3).

In other respects, however, the book of Daniel speaks of relations with Hellenism in different terms. From now on there is no longer any need to persuade the reader to mistrust the new culture: its malevolent character is evident. At any rate at the level of the final redaction, it is no longer a time for guarding against or refuting the arguments of the adversary: it is a time of violent confrontation. In human terms the situation of believers is desperate, and yet YHWH remains the master of history; at a fixed time, when evil seems to be triumphing over good, the God of Israel will bring the turning point and give victory to his faithful for ever. That is God's great secret, of which all are ignorant except the one to whom he has revealed it.

The adversary of the believers is Yavan (8.21; 10.20), i.e. Greece, or rather Hellenism. But in fact the combat goes far beyond human forces: in it the God of Israel is facing the empire of evil, of which the Seleucid king is merely the last incarnation. The dream of the composite statue (ch.2) shows this well: it is the whole of paganism, with its successive empires, which is overthrown by God at the moment when it proves to be most aggressive. The action of the forces of darkness is part of a precise plan: to force all men and women to worship the prince of evil (3.4–5, 10; 6.8, 13) and exterminate without mercy those who refuse (3.6, 11, 14–15; 6.8, 13); the victory of paganism is apparent in the profanation of the temple and its sacred vessels (5.2–4).

Thinking only of the human forces, the faithful will inevitably be defeated and exterminated: whatever their heroism, this battle is beyond them. God alone can come to their aid and win the victory. The one who holds his secrets can recognize in him the master of history: God has his plan which is unfolding implacably, unknown to the various human agents. Thus it is that those sent by God can announce in advance, with the help of different images, 'what must come to pass' (2.45): the succession of the four empires (chs. 2–7), but also in a more precise way the history of the world and of Israel, down to the Hellenistic period (the vision of the ram and the he-goat, ch. 8; the great vision of chs. 10–12). Nothing escapes the divine plan, not even the apparent defeat of his faithful.

In fact the whole of history is focussed on its end: 'Behold, I will make known to you what shall be at the latter end of the indignation; for it pertains to the appointed time for the end' (Dan. 8.19). The term is fixed (11.27, 35), the days are counted (8.14; 9.24–27; 2.11–12) and 'what is determined will be fulfilled' (11.56). This day will see the overthrow of the pagan empire, symbolized by the disappearance of the statue (2.35, 45), by the inscription in the palace of Belshazzar, whose kingdom is already 'measured' and 'weighed' and will soon be 'divided', or by the defeat of the fourth beast (7.26). The time of the end will see the inauguration of a new kingdom 'which will never be destroyed' (2.44), a kingdom entrusted 'to the people of the saints of the Most High' (7.27). Believers have only to remain faithful to the Law and to put their trust in God; he is the one who delivers (3.15, 17, 28, 29), just as he snatched the young men out of the furnace and Daniel from the lions' den (ch. 6). Thus the theology of the book of Daniel leads to a passive attitude in the face of events: it is enough to hold on faithfully and wait for the divine intervention.

The book of Daniel is the earliest of the apocalyptic writings. It inaugurates a literary genre which is better represented in the extra-biblical Jewish literature ('Ethiopian' Enoch, 'Slavonic' Enoch, the Apocalypse of Ezra, the Syriac Apocalypse of Baruch, etc.) than in the Bible itself (see above all the Apocalypse of John). However, other writings in the first Testament are comparable to Daniel in their fundamental orientation.

(a) Chapters 9–14 of the book of *Zechariah* ('Deutero-Zechariah') speak of the war which YHWH will wage to liberate Israel and assure his triumph. A recurrent theme is that of the pastors who have responsibility for the people of YHWH but do not care for their flock (10.2–3; 11.4–17; 13.7–9). This second part of the book of Zechariah was edited in the Hellenistic period.

Read Zech. 9; 11.4–17.

(b) The book of *Esther* tells how in the time of the Persian king Ahasuerus (Xerxes), the Jewish people had been threatened with extermination by the decision of the cruel Haman, and then saved by the exemplary conduct of Mordecai and Esther, who became the king's spouse. The narrative ends with the execution of Haman and the honouring of Mordecai, while the Jews massacre their enemies. The redaction of the book can be put in the second quarter of the second century. The ending, which relates the official institution of the Jewish feast of Purim (9.20–32) and is in praise of Mordecai (10.1–3), looks like an addition. The Greek translation contains important supplements.

Read Esther 4.1–17; 6.1–8.12.

(c) Like the book of Esther, the book of *Judith* – of which we have only the Greek version and other versions which derive from it – relates the miraculous deliverance of Israel thorough the action of a woman. The Jews are being besieged at Bethulia by the army of Holophernes, general of Nebuchadnezzar, 'king of the Assyrians'(!). Judith pretends to be a runaway and promises the general that she will give him the means of capturing the city. Holphernes takes Judith into his tent, but he is soon laid low by wine, and the heroine takes advantage of this to cut off his head. The next day the besiegers discover the corpse of their leader: seized with panic, they are wiped out by the Israelites. In this narrative the author is envisaging the events of the second century: Nebuchadnezzar represents Antiochus IV and Judith ('the Jewish woman') represents the Israelite people helped by its God. The book seems to have been written around the middle of the second century.

Read Judith 9; 12.10–13.20.

(d) The final redaction of the book of *Isaiah* can be situated in the same context. Chapters 24–27 and 34–35 are often called the Isaiah apocalypses. These sections of the book, in which the eschatological perspective is explicit, are in fact composite and the titles given to them are incorrect. Nevertheless, the book was supplemented in the Hellenistic era with a series of additions which interpret it in the direction of apocalyptic theology: 10.22ab–23; 24.16, 21–23, etc. In the last chapters of the book, late additions emphasize the 'extermination of the nation and the kingdom which will not serve (YHWH)' (60.12), while YHWH himself will be an eternal light for Israel (60.19–20). He will create new heavens and a new earth which will make Jerusalem rejoice (65.17–18a); the people of YHWH will enjoy extraordinary longevity (65.20, 22b), comparable to the eternity of the new heavens and the new earth (66.22).

The Book of Wisdom

The book of the Wisdom of Solomon represents original reflection by the Jewish community in Alexandria. The date of the work is open to question: the allusions to the cult of the emperor and to the *pax romana* (14.22) allow the best present-day scholars to suggest the period of Augustus or a little later (first half of the first century CE). At this time Alexandria was one of the greatest cities of the Roman empire; it was distinguished for its flourishing trade and the splendour of its intellectual life, as witnessed by its famous library, the development of the sciences and the prestige of its philosophical schools. It was also the most important centre of the Jewish Diaspora. The community benefitted from a special status and it too stood out for the fame of its intellectuals, chief of whom is Philo.

We can recognize in the book of Wisdom the Greek literary genre of the encomium or eulogy. Aristotle presents it in his *Rhetoric* as a speech about practising a virtue. It comprises an exordium aimed at attracting attention and presenting the theme of the speech, which also allows a say to the opponents of the thesis defended; then it criticizes them and shows from some amazing situations the vital importance of the value proposed: we find such an exordium in Wisdom 1–6. Then follows the eulogy proper, which aims to show the origin, the nature and the benefits of the value in question (here Wisdom 7–9). The last part offers an 'amplification' by means of examples which present a moral lesson; these examples are often presented in a comparison with well-known figures, to show the superiority of those who are being praised. This third part (here Wisdom 10–19), the content of which is freer and which can contain digressions, ends with a summary of the conclusions arrive at through the examples. Down to details, the book of Wisdom is constructed on these principles.

The book of Wisdom is based throughout on former scriptures

(Exodus, but also the Psalter, Isaiah, etc.) and Jewish tradition; its aim is to promote wisdom, 'the purest emanation of the glory of the all-powerful' (7.26). Nowhere do we find an explicit identification of wisdom with the Mosaic Torah, as in Sirach 24, but the author aims at faithfulness to this Law, to the will of the 'God of the Fathers' (Wisdom 9.1); the wise man is said to be 'righteous' (3.1, etc.) and the one who is not wise is called 'impious' (1.9, 16, etc.), 'blasphemer' (1.6) or 'sinner'. The author is addressing other Jews who are fired by Alexandrian Hellenism and its prestige, and in particular by the growing success of the mystery cults, astrology and Hermeticism. In the face of this competition from paganism and new forms, the author of the book of Wisdom wants to defend the Jewish traditions: the antitheses of the last chapters contrast the failure of Egypt (= Alexandrian paganism) with the favour granted to Moses (= loyalty to the Mosaic Torah). So its message can be put in a line with Sirach, with the same sense of divine retribution.

In content, the book of Wisdom is at the opposite pole from Koheleth; some scholars have even seen 2.1–9 as a critique of this work. However, like Koheleth it is steeped in Hellenistic culture, which it uses to bring out the traditional thought of Israel. As well as the use of the Greek language, several marks of the cultural influence of Hellenism are visible. The whole book is written in accordance with the artistic canons of Greek rhetoric, and more particularly the rules of the encomium. In literary genre, the work has no parallel in the Hebrew Bible. The vocabulary used is richer than that of the LXX; it allows a more abstract reflection than Hebrew. A whole series of other borrowings from Hellenism have been listed; for example, the four virtues listed in 8.7 are of a typically Stoic type.

The recourse to Hellenistic culture not only serves to expound traditional doctrine in a more attractive way; it also makes it possible to refine or extend it. That is the case with the discourse on immortality, which is influenced by various philosophical trends. Almost certainly basing himself on Neoplatonic doctrines, the author affirms that God has created human beings for incorruptibility (2.23; cf. 1.15); the devil made them mortal (2.24). The wise man – the one who lives according to the will of God – will benefit from this incorruptibility (6.18–19), while the impious will suffer eternal punishment (3.9–10). It is in the other world that the contradictions of the world will be overcome by divine justice.

The author of the book of Wisdom does more than translate traditional biblical thought into Greek: the contribution of Hellenism allows him to advance boldly along the course of his own tradition. He does not fuse the two cultures, but links them to defend the Israelite heritage in a pluralistic society. Today, no one dares any longer to write that the author is addressing pagan readers with a view to converting them to Judaism; besides, it seems that any idea of a Jewish proselytism had to be abandoned at this time. So if he is also witnessing to the pagan world, he is doing so indirectly. The fact remains that the type of Judaism of which the Wisdom of Solomon is an expression exerted some fascination on intellectual Alexandrian circles. This effort to inculturate the tradition in Hellenistic areas was to bear fruit: the Jewish community of Alexandria became lively and creative, particularly in the literary sphere.

Read Wisdom 7.22–9.18; 13–14.

Conclusion

Relations with culture are vitally important for any believing community. Faced with the challenge presented by the irresistible rise of a new and attractive culture, the Jewish communities were not unanimous. The canon of scripture contains books which defend different reactions: assimilation, condemnation in the name of the defence of traditional values, demonization, discernment and linkage. No solution was established beyond dispute. The Bible leaves the door open to different attitudes towards modern culture: it does not dictate any solution, but reminds readers of their own responsibilities.

Koheleth, Sirach, Daniel and the book of Wisdom were not written in the same circumstances. Koheleth is the first to speak out, doubtless at a time when Judaism did not yet feel truly threatened by the new culture; his point of view was accepted into the Jewish and Christian canons of scripture, but he also calls for observance of the commandments, and he remains an isolated case. The point of view of Sirach can be explained by the disquiet of believers attached to the tradition when faced with a movement of disaffection from the law and cultic practices. The violent reaction of the book of Daniel is brought about by an exceptional situation, that of the persecution of Antiochus IV. The openness of the book of Wisdom is possible only in a Diaspora community in which the minority status of Judaism calls for different choices from those of Jerusalem. Perhaps we should remember that there is no solution valid for all time, but that each particular situation calls for an appropriate response. Suggestions made in particular circumstances should not be absolutized.

We must note the different choices made by Judaism and rising Christianity. Judaism sweepingly favoured the way taken by Sirach, even if it did not accept the book. By contrast, Christianity adopted the solution of the book of Wisdom and moreover adopted the LXX, which stemmed from the same Alexandrian Judaism. As is attested by the book of Acts and the letters of Paul, the choice to open the church to Christians of pagan origin went along with a certain distancing from the Jewish Law (or at least from some of its aspects) and made the spirit of Sirach intolerable. The New Testament writings and then, quite clearly, those of the first church fathers, show how Christian faith expressed itself from the beginning by using the resources of Greek culture.

The different choices of Judaism and Christianity in relation to Hellenistic culture had immense consequences. The way in which Judaism turned in on its own heritage and its opposition to any alliance with the dominant culture became necessary after the drama of the first Jewish War: it is all the more understandable since Jews did not seek to convert pagans. This choice allowed Judaism to survive not only at that time, but down the centuries which followed, and despite a series of dramatic trials. When the threat became too pressing, the need for security prevailed over everything else. The opposite option taken by the church in the first century made it run important risks. This was a bold choice, which involved conflicts and was possible only through faith in the Holy Spirit. But finally, was it not this openness to Greek culture which allowed the rapid spread of Christianity through the Roman empire? If Christians had not integrated important elements of Hellenistic rhetoric and philosophy into their preaching, their word would have had only a limited impact and the gospel would not have spread to all peoples. So profound was the integration of the message of the gospel and Greek culture that to many Christians these two elements seem indissoluble. Today, however, the essentialism of ancient philosophy – of Aristotle in particular – has become alien to the majority of Westerners. Other cultures are gradually beginning to exert themselves, as Hellenism did formerly. Can Christianity express itself, in all fidelity, in categories which are no longer inherited from Greek thought but which integrate different cultural contributions? Beyond question, to a great extent the future of the Christian communities depends on the answer given to this question.

The Lamb

Why do Christians read what they call the 'Old Testament', when they have the novelty of the Gospel? How does their own experience as believers allow them to read this book differently? A scene from the Book of Revelation can help us to answer these questions. In the heavenly liturgy of chs. 4 and 5 God holds in his right hand a scroll 'written within and on the back' and sealed with seven seals (5.1). Several recent commentaries explain – and they are almost certainly right – that this book is the Old Testament of the Christians. The book is closed. In other words, people know the Bible, but they can decipher only the external appearance. Only the Lamb who is slain yet standing – Jesus Christ risen, bearing the marks of his passion – is worthy to break the seals and to reveal to the world the full scope of the text. The definitive key to the scriptures is held by Christ, who is their interpreter *par excellence*. From now on it is impossible to read the book without being guided and enlightened by the Lamb.

Read Rev. 4–5.

In fact, the Book of Revelation presents itself throughout as a vast and ambitious re-reading of the scriptures, from Genesis on. Everything that has been announced or sketched out finds its fulfilment here. So, for example, the book ends with the final victory over the Beast (ch. 20) and the vision of the new heavens and the new earth, with the heavenly Jerusalem (chs. 21–22); here we can recognize the images of Gen. 1, taken to their final fulfilment. With the victory of Christ, everything is renewed. This was the intense experience of the first Christian generation.

If everything is new, why go back to the Old? From the first half of the second century, voices were raised in the church in opposition to the use of the first Testament. In Rome, Marcion thought that Jesus Christ had come to inaugurate a new world, and that one should no longer dwell on the old one, which had now perished. He understood the God of the Old Testament as a God of fear, while Jesus had revealed a God of love. Similarly, some Gnostic scriptures rejected the use of scripture outside strictly Christian writings. Indeed the Marcionite tendency to reject or forget the first Testament is a permanent one in the churches, as is attested by the often very small space given to the Hebrew Bible in catechesis and preaching. It is a fact that despite some progress, Catholics are largely ignorant of what comes before the Gospels. However, we must remember that Marcion was not followed by the church; the Christian communities have always maintained the need, at least theoretically, to read the Bible from Genesis to the book of Revelation, the Christian Apocalypse. We need to see continuity rather than a break between the Bible of Israel, Jesus and Christian experience. The two Testaments together form a single history through which God gives himself to human beings and reveals his face. There is a logical progression: the Old Testament is the order of prefiguration, promise, the announcement of an event to come, while the New Testament is the order of realization or fulfilment. This is a committed reading: at the centre of the perspective is faith in Jesus Christ, who has come to inaugurate the kingdom of God, and it is in terms of this essential faith that from now on everything is seen and assessed.

Given that, the relationship between the two Testaments continues to raise questions. It can be looked at from more than one perspective. Let's being by noting a fact: the writings of the New Testament say that Jesus died and rose 'according to the scriptures'. Then we can reflect on the apologetic presentation of Jesus as the one who corresponds to the portrait painted by the 'messianic texts' of the first Testament. Finally, we can see how the link between the two Testaments proceeds from a double movement: the first disciples could only understand the mystery of Christ by meditating on the scriptures; conversely, the event of Christ invites us to re-read the whole book in a renewed perspective.

'According to the scriptures'

This is one of the major axes of Christian reflection on the 'harmony of the two Testaments': the Old announces and prepares for the New. The Gospels already point us in this direction. 'Today this passage of scripture is fulfilled in your ears,' declares Jesus after reading Isa. 61 in the synagogue of Nazareth (Luke 4.21). Similarly, in one of his appearances after Easter, Jesus declares: 'Everything written about me in the law of Moses and the prophets and the psalms must be fulfilled' (Luke 24.44). After the Last Supper, Jesus says to the Twelve: 'You will all fall away; for it is written, "I will strike the shepherd and the sheep will be scattered" (Mark 14.27, quoting Zech. 13.7). The formulae in the Gospel of Matthew are also typical: 'all this happened that the prophecy of the Lord might be fulfilled . . .' (Matt. 1.22; cf. 2.15, 16, 23; 4.14, etc.). Along the same lines we may note the importance of the argument from scripture in the speeches in the Acts of the Apostles, relating to the passion and the resurrection (Acts 2.16–21, 25–31, 34–35, etc.). A very old creed of the church is quoted by Paul: 'Christ died for our sins according to the scriptures. He was buried, he was raised on the third day according to the scriptures. He appeared to Cephas...' (I Cor. 15.3–5). This text quotes a traditional formula which is earlier than Paul himself. The reference to the scriptures – in fact the first Testament – here is massive. Moreover, every expression has its roots in the first Testament: 'Christ' refers to the *māšiāh* or Messiah of many texts; 'died for our sins' echoes Isa.53.4; 'risen the third day' recalls Hos. 6.2.

So everything that concerns Jesus took place 'according to the scriptures'. Or, in other words, Jesus fulfils the scriptures. But how are we to understand these formulae? We need to take account of two complementary lines: only the reading of the scriptures allows us to understand Jesus Christ; on the other hand, it is the 'event of Jesus Christ' which provides the final meaning of these same scriptures.

The scriptures, 'proof' of Jesus?

'Jesus fulfils the scriptures.' This statement is often understood in an apologetic sense: Jesus corresponds to the portrait of the Messiah painted by the Old Testament, which proves the truth of the Christian faith. Such a use of the Bible probably goes back to the first Jewish-Christian polemic. It seems that in the first century lists were made of texts which were considered messianic, in particular some psalms (2; 22; 110, etc.) and a certain number of prophetic texts. Is this way of reading the Bible legitimate?

The messianic hope is one of the facts of the history of Israel, and the Bible broadly echoes it. Again we have to take the expression in a very wide sense: not the precise expectation of the coming of Jesus but the hope of new, glorious and happy times promised by God. The promises of the first Testament outline the features of a world in which YHWH, victorious over the forces of evil hostile to Israel, fully exercises his reign in peace and justice. The main hope of the Jewish world is not the Messiah as such but the kingdom of God, and it is the dawn of this kingdom or reign that Jesus announces in his preaching and begins to realize by his acts of salvation (healings and exorcisms, the forgiveness of sins, the reintegration of the outcast). In this very widest sense Jesus fulfils what had been announced, or rather he gives the first signs of it, since the full realization of the kingdom is still to come. Jesus gives signs, not proofs; only in faith is it possible to recognize the breaking in of the kingdom.

The Hebrew Bible often speaks of the *māšiāh*, 'anointed', a term rendered by the word 'Messiah'. In texts prior to the exile (e.g. Ps. 2), we do not have an ideal sovereign still to come, but quite simply a king who was anointed when he succeeded to power. This king is presented in accordance with the conventions of the royal ideology. After the collapse of the monarchy, these texts were reinterpreted. At one time it was possible to read into them a promise of the restoration of the monarchy, in the person of Zerubbabel. When this hope disappeared in its turn, the symbolism of the *māšiāh* was transferred to the high priest or, in other texts, to the believing community of Jerusalem, the 'city of David', heir to the promises about him (II Sam. 7.1–16). Messianism as the expectation of an ideal king who will save Israel at

the end of time does not appear in the Bible, and the prophets themselves were never aware that they were proclaiming the coming of a
distant Messiah. Such an expectation is attested in the time of Jesus,
but outside the text of the Bible. John the Baptist's question, 'Are you
he who is to come, or are we to look for another?' (Matt. 11.3), is thus
topical. Jewish society was in a messianic ferment, linked to a very
lively sense of eschatology: the one who was to come would hold a
universal judgment and inaugurate a new order for the whole world.
However, the hesitations of John the Baptist, like the attitude of the
crowds, show that Jesus did not correspond to the portrait that the
scriptures painted of the Messiah. To the scribes and Pharisees who
asked for a sign – probably a sign to accredit him as Messiah – Jesus
replied: 'An evil and adulterous generation seeks for a sign; but no sign
shall be given to it except the sign of the prophet Jonah' (Matt. 12.39;
cf. 16.4). There is still much discussion of the nature of this 'sign of
Jonah'; the most probable interpretation is that it is a 'counter-sign'
formed by the death of Jesus. Be this as it may, it is useless to seek
proof of the messiahship of Jesus. The first Testament cannot be
reduced to a descriptive announcement of Jesus. We must seek other
ways of understanding its relationship to the New Testament.

Scripture, the key to understanding Jesus

'Who do you say that I am?' The question resounds through the
Gospels. And indeed Jesus was an enigma for his contemporaries.
Those who encountered him and became his disciples were impressed
by his manner of being, of speaking, of living. Otherwise they would
not have followed him. But only very gradually did they perceive the
depth of his mystery. How was one to understand Jesus? Even during
his ministry, responses were being sketched out. Was he a prophet,
like John the Baptist? Or the Prophet *par excellence,* Elijah, whose
return was awaited? Could he be the Messiah, the king and saviour,
son of David, sent by God? The Emmanuel of Isa. 7.14? Or again the
mysterious 'Son of man' spoken of in Dan. 7? All these titles given to
Jesus come from the Hebrew Bible. To understand the mystery of
Jesus, those who encountered him reacted as people had done all

through the history of Israel: they looked for an answer in scripture. Which of these titles did Jesus himself use? The question is a tricky one, since it is hardly possible to plumb the depths of his mind, and the Gospels project the light of Easter on to the pre-Easter Jesus. Again, meditation on scripture has gradually made some response to the enigma possible. In the episode on the Emmaus road, Jesus himself invites such reading: 'And he said to them, "O foolish men, and slow of heart to believe all that the prophets have spoken! Was it not necessary that the Christ should suffer these things and enter into his glory?" and beginning with Moses and the prophets he interpreted to them in all the scriptures the things concerning himself' (Luke 24.25–27).

The enigma, presented from the beginning of the public activity of Jesus, recurs decisively after the passion and the experience of Easter. No one will be surprised that a prophet is rejected and even condemned to death. But the Messiah? And what does the experience of the resurrection mean for the mystery of Jesus? Once again, it is reading the book which has progressively made it possible to formulate answers. Here some texts have played a key role: the songs of the suffering servant of Isa. 40–55; the psalms of the righteous sufferer (Ps. 22, for example), but also various eschatological and apocalyptic texts (especially Daniel, Zechariah and Malachi). It was reflection on scripture in the light of the Easter experience that led the Christian community to discover, to its surprise – for Jewish monotheism might seem absolutely to forbid it – the divinity of Jesus. It is by confessing Jesus as Son of God that one does justice to his mystery.

Jesus Christ, the key to understanding scripture

It is impossible to understand Jesus without reading and re-reading the scriptures. Conversely, the encounter with Jesus Christ leads to a new understanding of the whole of the Book. In inaugurating the kingdom and thus realizing God's great promise, Jesus is opening up a major new development. But the rising Christian community discovered that everything that had gone before prepared for Jesus.

'Think not that I have come to abolish the law and the prophets: I have come not to abolish them but to fulfil them' (Matt. 5.17). So Jesus 'fulfils' the scriptures. In what sense? We could understand this to mean that what had been announced was at last being realized. So the fulfilment would relate above all to the promises. Certainly the promises, even those which had already been realized (like the promise of descendants or the promise of the land made to Abraham), find a deeper fulfilment in him. But Jesus fulfils all the scriptures, and not just some chosen pages. The use of the term 'fulfil' suggests both fundamental continuity and novelty, resulting in a 'finality', the arrival at a summit.

The Old Testament is not content to announce the New, as if from the outside. Already, in various areas it sketches it out:

– This is true of the progressive discovery of monotheism, of God's goodness, of the prophetic preaching, covenant relations, the resurrection of the dead and other spiritual or theological achievements. Jesus would have been incomprehensible without all these advances.
– It is true of the quality of commitment shown by a number of believers to whom the Bible bears witness. Several characters of the Old Testament announce Jesus Christ by the witness of their own lives: thus the group speaking in Isa. 53 ('we') of a mysterious servant of God doubtless had in mind the believing community of Jerusalem, which had in fact accepted suffering to obtain the conversion and salvation of its brothers and sisters. It was not from the outside but by their very life that these people sketched out what Jesus would later accomplish.
– This is again true of the phenomenon of typology. Over long centuries Israel learned to read prefigurements of new events in its scriptures. When the novelty was a major one, the whole book underwent an unprecedented interpretation. Thus everything in the Bible becomes a figure of Christ: not only the characters (Adam, Abraham, Moses, David, the prophets . . .), but also the narratives (the flood, the Passover, the miracle of the Sea . . .).

For the Christian reader, it is in the death of Jesus on the cross and the experience of encounter with the risen Christ that the Bible reaches its climate, from which everything is illuminated and restructured. The new reading of the whole of the Bible provoked by the Christian experience has been represented in a splendid sculpture at Vézelay, called 'The Mystical Mill'. Moses, wearing the short garment of slaves, is pouring in the good grain of the Word, which is being received by Paul, dressed in the long robe of free men. We should note that this work of art at the same time expresses the ambiguity of the relations between Christians and Israel: the slaves harvest grain for bread which will be taken from their mouths by 'free' men. This could remind us of the episode of the marriage feast at Cana (John 2.1–12): the water 'intended for the purification of the Jews', represents the Law of Moses, which is going to give place to the wine of the feast, for the banquet of the kingdom. Water is indispensable to life; the encounter with Christ does not make it useless but transforms it.

The Christian reading of the Hebrew Bible cannot claim any exclusiveness: it does not do away with previous readings, but suggests a new interpretation which discovers a level of unforeseen meaning in the text. In other words, to forget their original scope and the readings made of them in the Israelite tradition would be to mutilate these texts.

Epilogue

This short book began with the narrative of the sending out of spies to reconnoitre the Promised Land. Like them, we have gone on a journey, discovered various landscapes and tasted the fruits of the country. Like them, too, we can say: 'We came to the land to which you sent us; it flows with milk and honey, and this is its fruit' (Num. 13.27). The Bible is revealed in its multiplicity and in its unity. I hope that our ten keys have allowed us to discover many treasures. Not only memories of the past, original cultures of former times to which we are the heirs, but also a word which brought life and continues to bring life. The road has been a long one. It may have seemed rough, since there have been plenty of obstacles. Not all the crossroads have been marked as clearly as they might have been. But those who have attempted the adventure and have now reached the end should have been rewarded for their efforts: beyond the words, perhaps they have been able to hear how God himself speaks to the heart of believers. The most important thing is not the explanation given through these pages, but reading of the Bible itself.

A first exploration is at an end. In the book of Numbers the explorers are not tourists, satisfied with bringing back photographs for their albums. They did not enter the land out of curiosity, but as the advance guard of a people called to live there. The sequel to the biblical narrative recalls how the people, in fear, refused this stay, thus condemning themselves to wandering in the wilderness; only the next generation dared to take the step, to live long days in this beautiful country. So a first exploration is over. But more needs to be done. May each reader live long in the land of the Bible, discovering for herself or himself – alone or, if possible with others – its riches and harvesting its fruits! There is always something new to discover. Even in passages which we have read a hundred times there will be always something new to glean: a precious pearl, a hidden treasure, food for the mind, for the heart, for faith and hope.

Finally, steeping oneself in the Bible isn't everything. The biblical testimony sends readers back to their own lives. We have to live, enriched by our reading.

Answers to questions in the boxes on pp. 56–61

p. 56

The three texts tell the story of the patriarch's wife, who goes into a foreign country. She is so beautiful that she arouses the desire of the king and puts her husband in great danger. So they decide to introduce themselves as brother and sister. Each time the situation is discovered, but the patriarch and his wife end up deriving advantage from it. The essentials of the scenario are common to the three texts. However, we need to note a series of differences. Here are the most striking of them:

– Different characters and places: we have Abraham and Sarah with the Pharaoh (ch. 12), Abraham and Sarah with Abimelech (ch. 20), and Isaac and Rebecca with Abimelech (ch. 26). From this perspective, ch. 20 is a kind of 'middle term' between the other two narratives.
– The trick is discovered by various means: scourges sent by YHWH (ch. 12), a dream (ch. 20), observation of the amorous gestures of the patriarchs (ch. 26).
– The order in which the story is told differs: only the first narrative introduces a dialogue between the patriarch and his wife before they arrive in the foreign land.
– The narrative in ch. 20 stands out in two ways: on the one hand we find the divine name 'Elohim' (in most Bibles translated 'God') in it four times, whereas it is absent from the other texts; on the other hand, the narrative has an ethical dimension (the question of guilt) which the others ignore.

There are different more or less probable explanations of these facts: reminiscences of comparable episodes, different developments of the oral tradition of an old narrative, literary dependence, and so on. Of the three parallel episodes, that of ch. 26 seems to be the most archaic: one can hardly explain a transition from the famous (Abraham, Pharaoh) to the obscure (Isaac, Abimelech).

p. 56

In vv. 5–8 the divine name is YHWH. Verses 9–13 restate the same divine decision to destroy guilty humankind but speak of Elohim (God).

p. 57

The question raised in 6.12 is answered in 7.1–5; this confirms the same link in 4.10–16. That raises at least two questions. What is the relationship between ch. 4 and chs. 6–7? What about 6.13–30, which interrupt the natural thread of the narrative?

p. 59

Joseph is the man of Hebron (37.14), like David. His older brothers are at Shechem (37.12, 13, 14), the symbolic centre of Israel in the North. They want to eliminate Joseph, but their action only leads them to prostrate themselves before him (42.6; cf. 37.7). In the context of the tenth century, the narrative could indicate that the tribes of Saul's old kingdom did not have to revolt against David, their new master: to want to eliminate him would only serve to confirm his power.

p. 60

Before the murder Cain is dominant: he is given by YHWH, he is the older, he is a landowner, and Abel, whose name means 'mist', 'nebulous', is described in relation to him, as if Cain were the well known great figure ('his brother'). After the murder, Abel occupies the land with his blood and Cain is chased out of it, taking the place of his younger brother. It is no use wanting to oppose the divine decisions: the murder only aggravates the situation. In other words, the accession of Solomon to the throne cannot be contested – even if the human rules would designate his older brother Adonijah.

p. 60

The two narratives of the expulsion of Hagar and Ishmael mention YHWH (ch. 16) and Elohim (ch. 12) respectively. In the first narrative Abraham is an accomplice in the brutal treatment of Hagar. In the second, however, he has scruples: if he sends Hagar away, it is with God's agreement and he does so gently (v.14). The Elohistic author takes up the J narrative, but corrects the behaviour of the patriarchs in a more moral direction.

p. 61

The destruction of Sodom prefigures that of Jerusalem. YHWH would have spared the city had it had some just men in it. The calamity which befalls Jerusalem can only be explained by the guilt of all his inhabitants: YHWH cannot be accused of injustice.

p. 61
See pp. 129f.